Spirituality in Art

Artwork of Jindrich Degen

Arranged by Eva and Alex Peck

Artwork: Jindrich Degen
Photography: Jindrich Degen, Alex Peck
Photo editing: Jindrich Degen, Eva Peck, Alex Peck
Text: Jindrich Degen, Eva Peck, Alex Peck
Design: Eva Peck, assisted by Alex Peck
Cover design: Eva and Alex Peck

National Library of Australia Cataloguing-in-Publication entry
Creator: Degen, Jindrich (Henry), 1923-
Title: Spirituality in art: artwork of Jindrich Degen / Jindrich
Degen; Eva and Alex Peck.

ISBN: 9780992454920 (paperback)

Subjects: Degen, Jindrich (Henry), 1923-
        Art, Abstract – Australia.
        Spirituality in art.

Other Creators/Contributors:
        Peck, Eva, compiler.
        Peck, Alex, compiler.

Dewey Number: 709.94

This book can be purchased online through http://www.henrydegen.com
or http://www.pathway-publishing.org. Also available at Amazon, Ingram
and other outlets worldwide

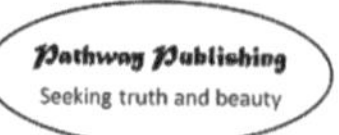

To Dad,
who in his 92nd year of life keeps busy
and is still remarkably creative.

Other Books Featuring Jindrich Degen's Work

Artistic Inspirations: Paintings of Jindrich Degen, arranged by Eva and Alexander Peck (2011)

Colour and Contrast: Artwork of Jindrich Degen, arranged by Eva and Alexander Peck (2013)*

Faces and Forms Across Time: Artwork of Jindrich Degen, arranged by Eva and Alexander Peck (2013)*

Variations: Art Exhibition of Jindrich Degen, arranged by Eva and Alex Peck (2013)

Nature in Art: Artwork of Jindrich Degen, arranged by Eva and Alex Peck (2014)*

Floral and Nature Art: Photography of Jindrich Degen, arranged by Eva and Alexander Peck (2011)

Nature's Beauty: Photography of Jindrich Degen, arranged by Eva and Alex Peck (2013)

Volné verše, Jindrich Degen (poetry in Czech, 2012)*

Verše pro dnešní dobu, Jindrich Degen (poetry in Czech, 2011)

The above books can be viewed and purchased online:
www.henrydegen.com
www.pathway-publishing.org
* Also available through
Amazon, Ingram, and other worldwide outlets.

CONTENTS

Spirituality in Abstract Art:
A Historical Glimpse

Back in 1911, several artists, including August Macke, Franz Marc, and Wassily Kandinsky, formed a German Expressionist group called *Der Blaue Reiter* (or The Blue Rider). These artists were dedicated to bringing to light spiritual truths in contemporary, and often abstract, art.

The Russian artist and art theorist, Wassily Kandinsky (1866-1944), was a pioneer of abstract art and expressive in his writings on the role of spirituality in art. His book, *Concerning the Spiritual in Art* (1912), continues to be valuable reading for artists and art students. In the book, Kandinsky discusses, among other topics, the effects of colours, including the spiritual effect. Blue, for example, is a colour of spirituality, or a celestial colour that evokes a deep calm.

German painter, Franz Marc (1880-1916), created the work *Gebirge* (Mountains, 1911-12) which conveys the impression of a path through jagged mountains. This path leads to the orange sun at the summit and is a spiritual metaphor for striving toward a higher realm.

August Macke (1887-1914) was another leading member of the group *Der Blaue Reiter*, sharing in their mystical and symbolic interests.

To send light into the darkness of men's hearts —

such is the duty of the artist.

~ Robert Schumann

INTRODUCTION

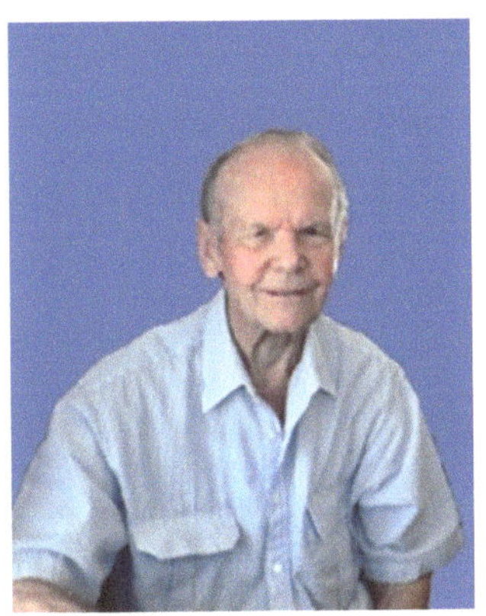

Born in 1923 in Prague, Czechoslovakia, Jindrich (Henry) Degen has enjoyed artwork since his childhood and adolescence. However, after his secondary education, he pursued his other great interest, music, following in the footsteps of his father, Jindrich Degen (1885-1972), cor anglais player in the Czech Philharmonic Orchestra.

From 1943 until 1979, Jindrich (Henry) Degen performed as principal oboist in various symphony and opera orchestras in Prague (now Czech Republic), Gothenburg (Sweden), and Melbourne (Victoria, Australia). He also produced educational music for the oboe which was published in Prague, England and Germany.

After his retirement in 1979, Jindrich moved from Victoria to Queensland where he began to fully devote himself to art. He took a four-year art course at the Sunshine Coast Institute of TAFE (Technical and Further Education). Later in the Redland City area, as a member of the Yurara Art Society, he attended workshops conducted by prominent artists, such as Irene Amos, Jan Jefferies, Jack Oudyn, and Michael John Taylor.

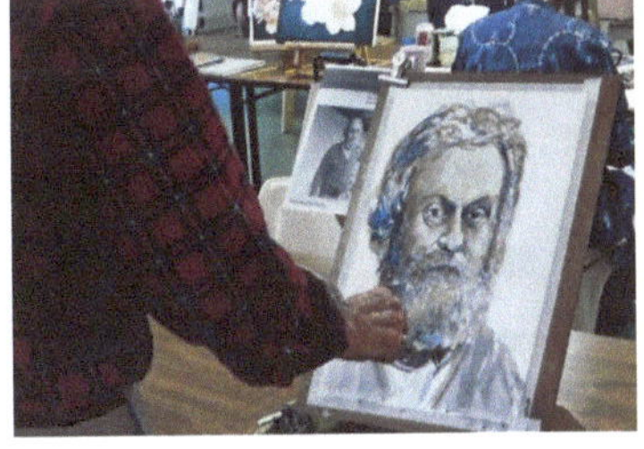

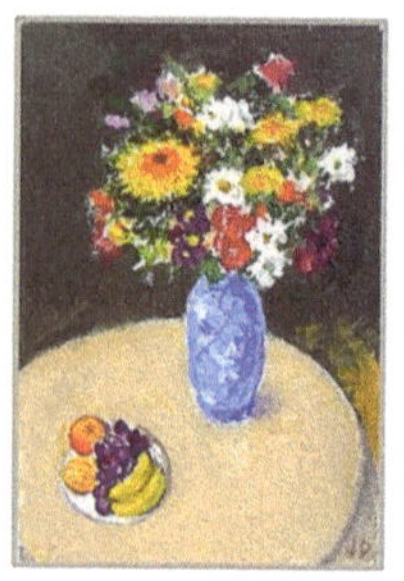

Jindrich's subject repertoire for his art is amazingly diverse. He likes painting realistic subjects, such as portraits, townscapes, still lifes, and nature themes. Yet he also enjoys colourful semi-abstract or abstract art, where he seeks to express his subconscious feelings in images using various media (such as oil, acrylic, pastel, and watercolour). Many of these works can be seen on his website www.henrydegen.com, as well as in earlier publications entitled *Artistic Inspirations* (2011); *Colour and Contrast* (2013); *Faces and Forms Across Time* (2013); and *Nature in Art* (2014). The artwork on the website and in these books highlights Jindrich's remarkable productivity and creativity in his later years.

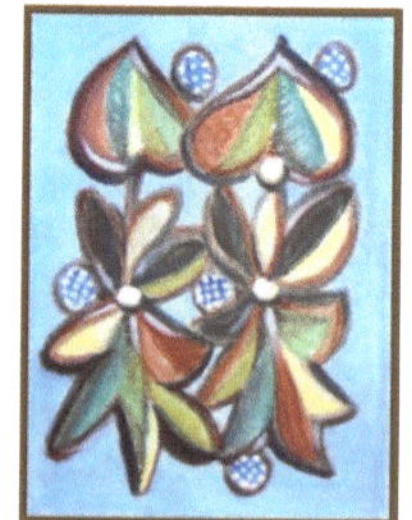

A respected local artist, Jindrich continues to take part in various art activities and exhibitions, especially those of the Yurara Art Society. During March-April 2004, he had a solo exhibition, entitled *Images and Inventions*, in the Redland Art Gallery, Cleveland. In July-August 2010, in an exhibition entitled *Mandala Inspiration*, he displayed a selection of his mandala paintings at the same gallery. In November 2013, he had a solo exhibition entitled *Variations* at the Yurara Art Society Gallery in Thornlands.

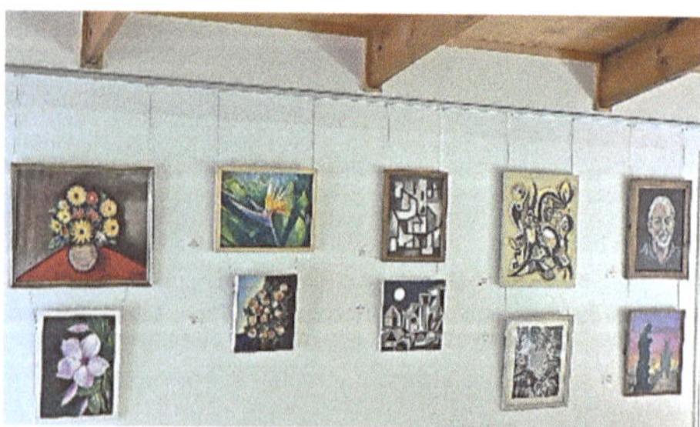

Another solo exhibition, entitled *Contrasts,* is scheduled for July-September 2015 at the Redland Art Gallery, Capalaba.

Introduction

This latest book featuring forty-four of Jindrich's works is a selection of paintings relating to themes of spirituality. It represents his artistic endeavours over more than a decade. The collection contains mainly abstract art and is organized under six themes – enlightenment, spiritual journey, meditation, mandalas, Christian symbolism, and celebration.

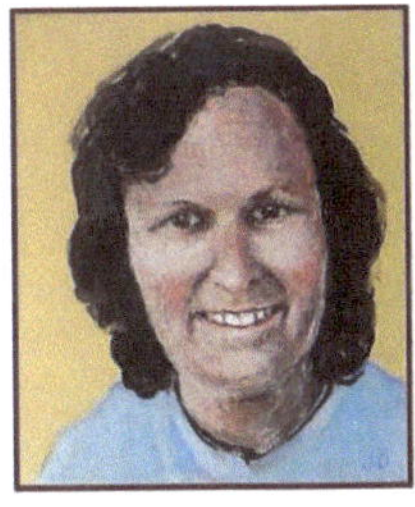

Jindrich's daughter, Eva, arranged this collection of artwork with assistance from her husband, Alex. Jindrich supplied the photographs of his works with their specifications. He also painted the portraits of his daughter and son-in-law featured on this page.

Jindrich's desire is that the images in this latest collection will leave visitors to his "gallery in print" uplifted and inspired.

Eva and Alex Peck

February 2015

*A spiritual search in art is looking for meaning
outside of yourself.*
~ Ross Bleckner

Creativity is the voice of the spirit.
One's art should be the extension of oneself.
~ Maritza Burgos

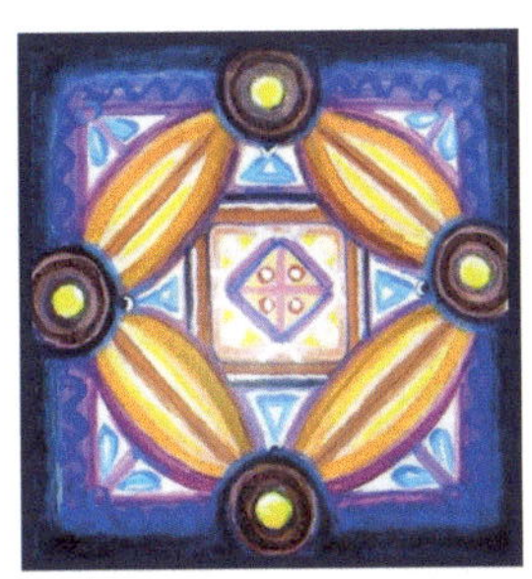

Enlightenment

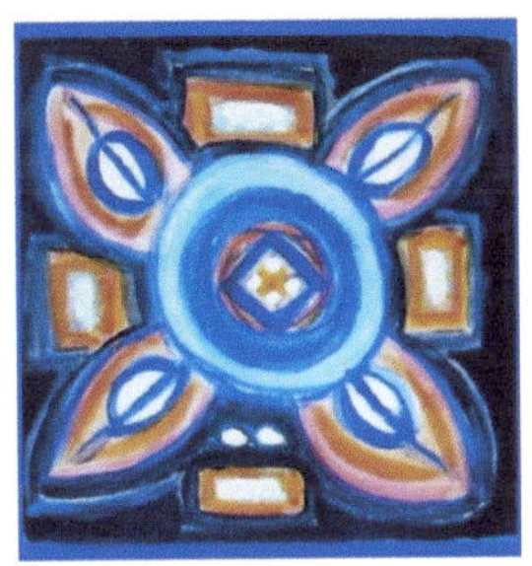

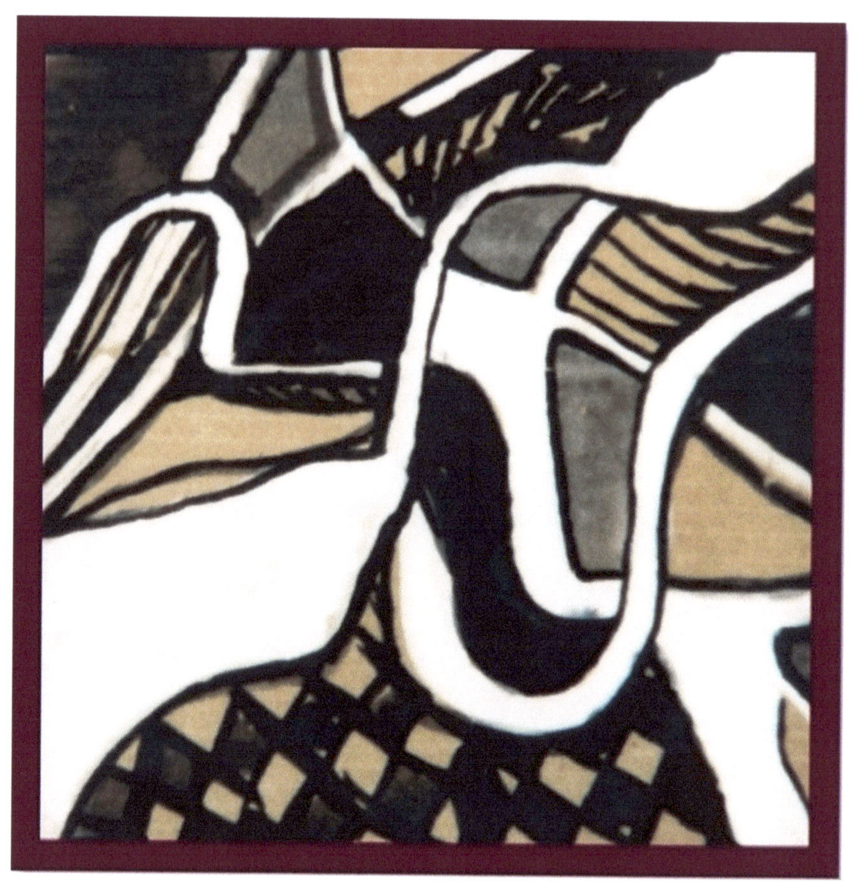

Different Ways

Acrylic on paper, 27 x 27 cm, 2002

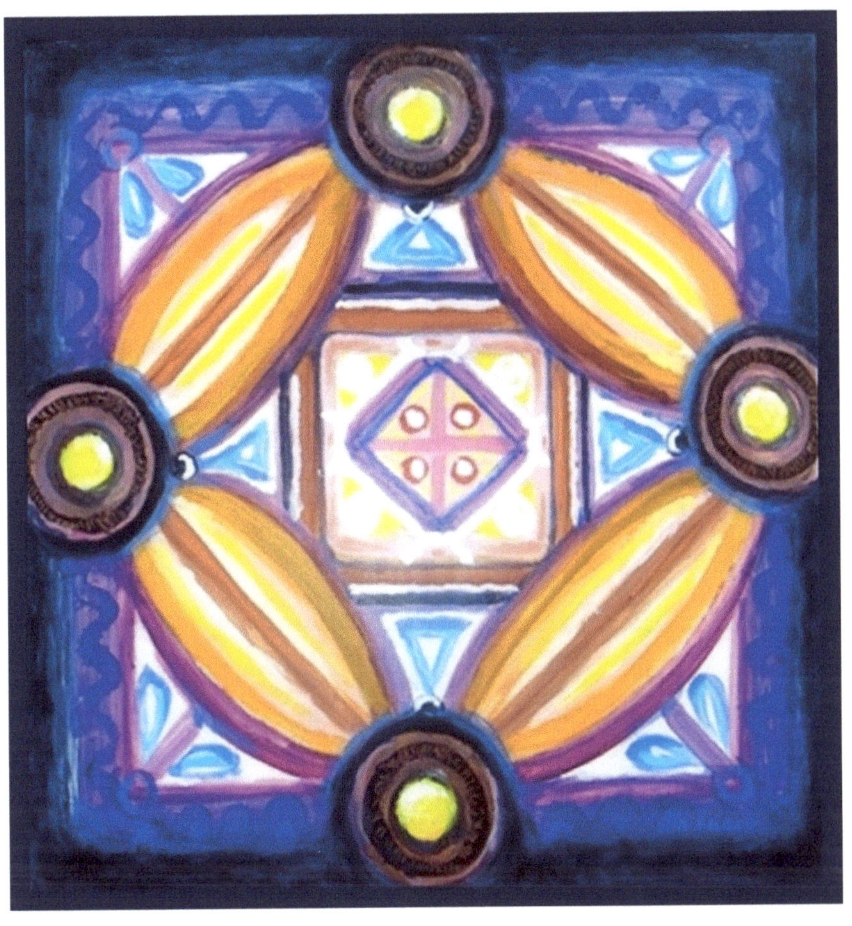

Message

Acrylic on board, 60 x 59 cm, 2010

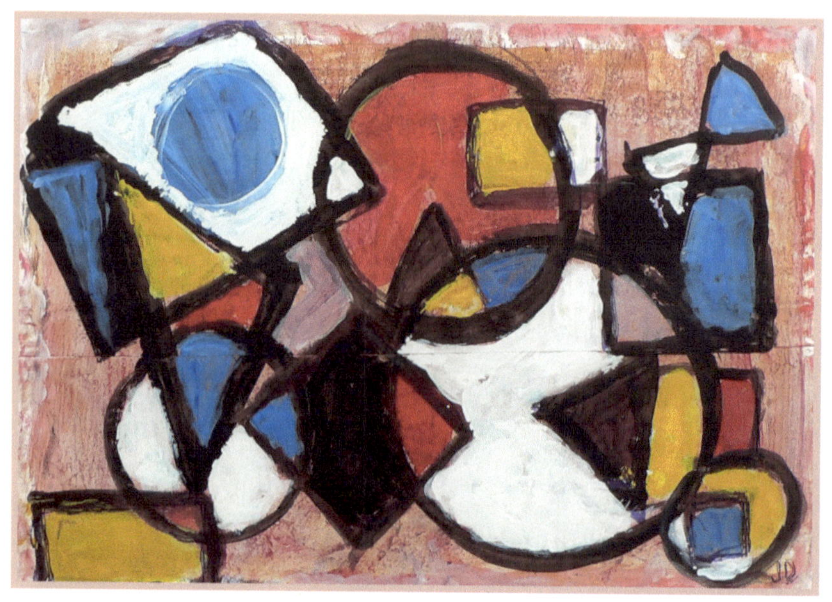

Strong Encounter

Acrylic on paper, 22 x 30 cm, 2003

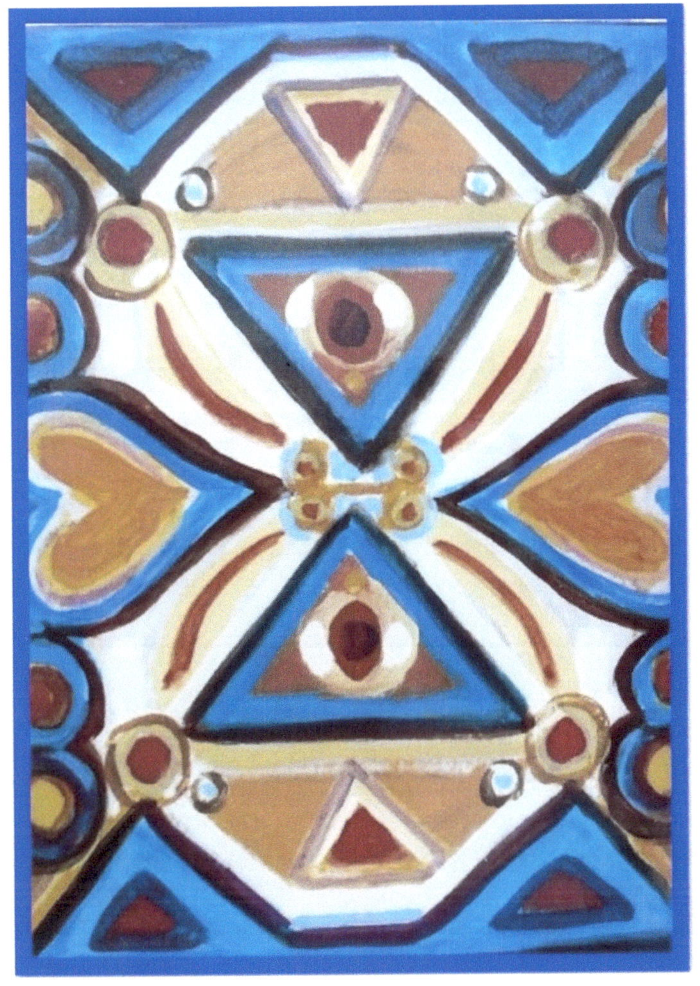

Awakening

Acrylic on board, 54 x 41 cm, 2008

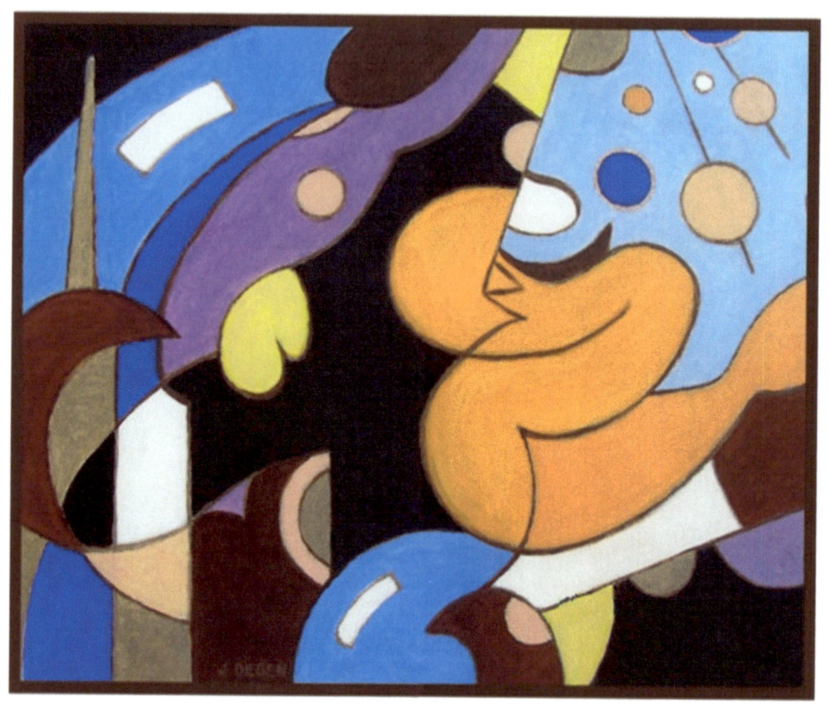

View in the Dark

Acrylic on canvas, 61 x 76 cm, 2009

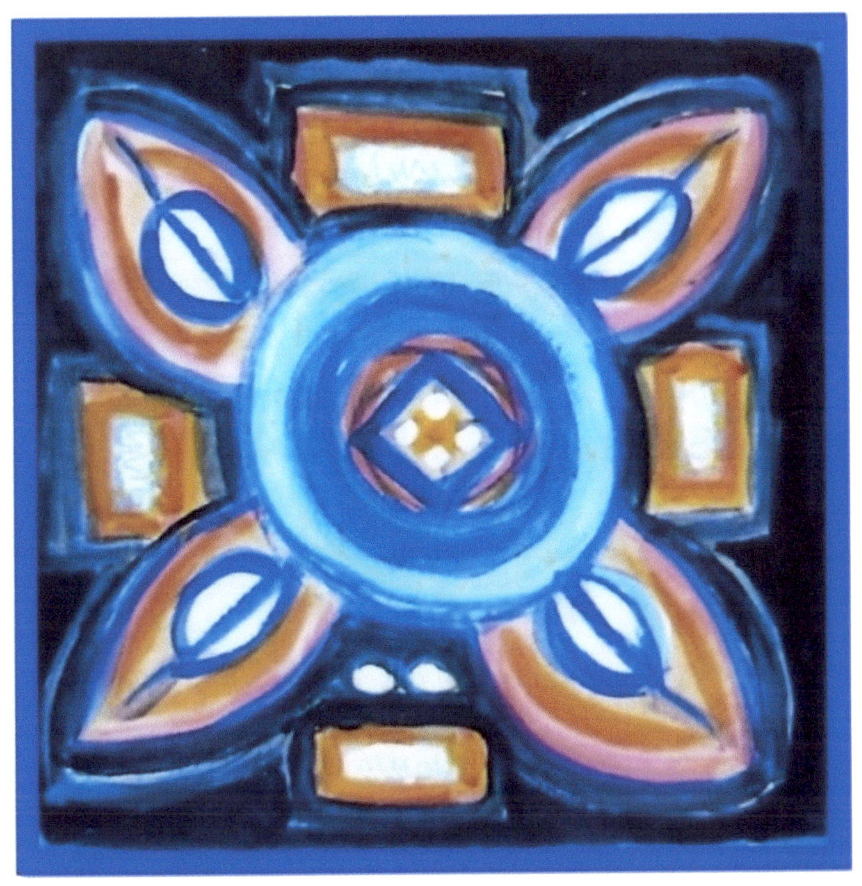

Clear Sight

Acrylic on paper, 27 x 27 cm, 2004

*Painting is an art, and art is not vague production,
transitory and isolated, but a power
which must be directed to the improvement and
refinement of the human soul.*
~ Wassily Kandinsky

*Art becomes a spiritual process depending upon
the degree of commitment that you bring to it.
Every experience becomes direct food for your art.
Then your art teaches you about life.*
~ Nick Bantock

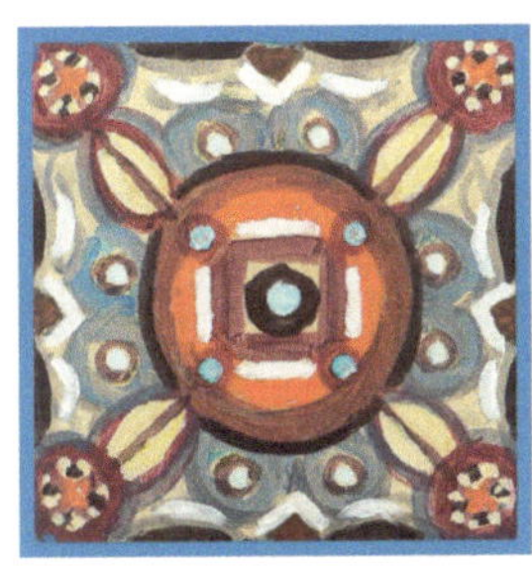

Spiritual Journey

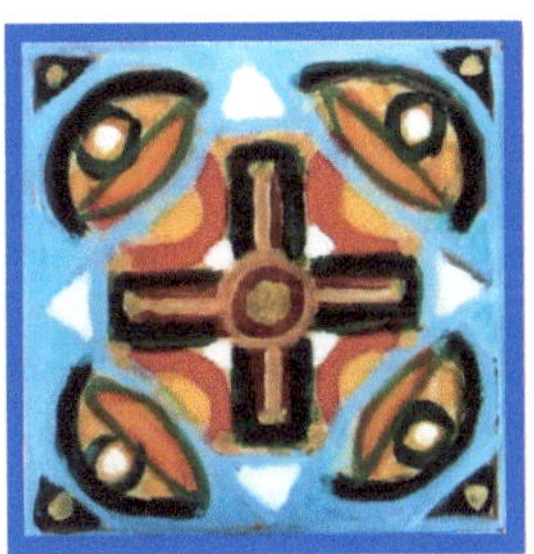

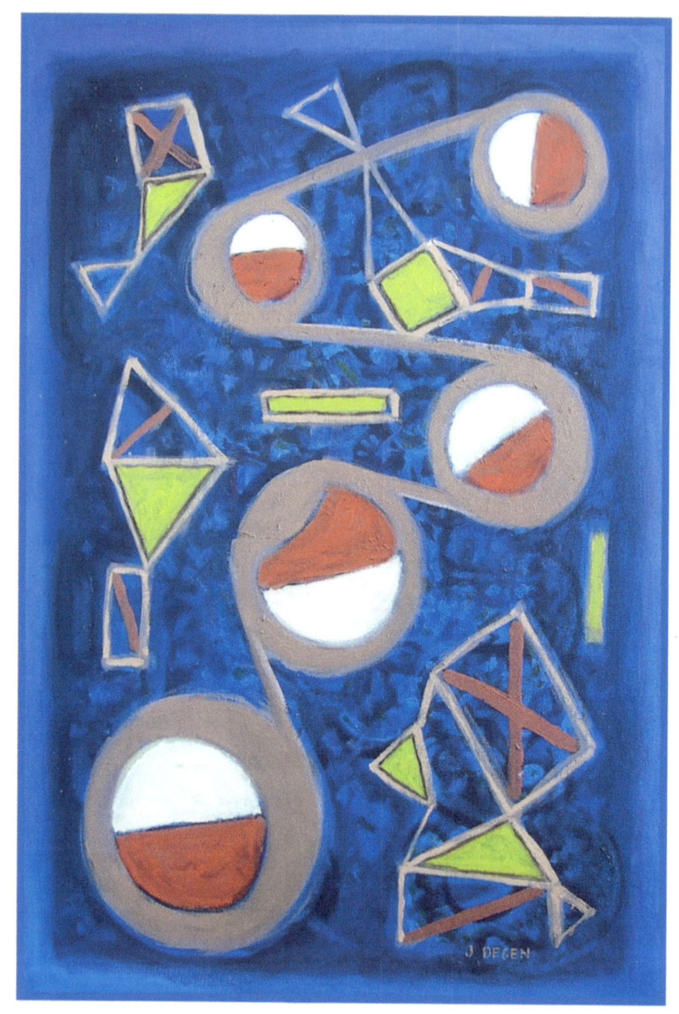

Good Message

Oil on canvas, 75 x 51 cm, 2003

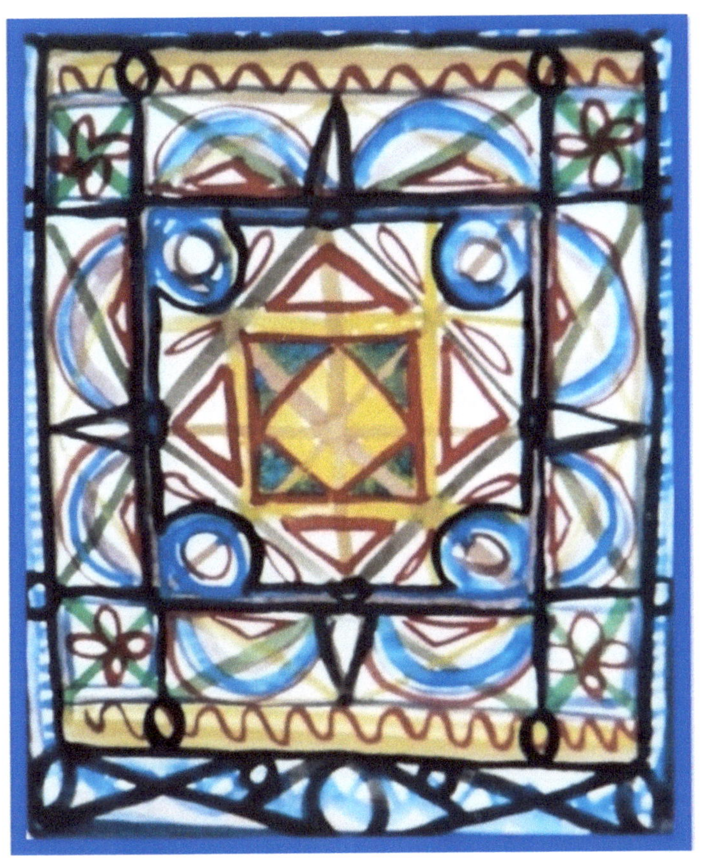

The Hope

Acrylic on paper, 32 x 28 cm, 2007

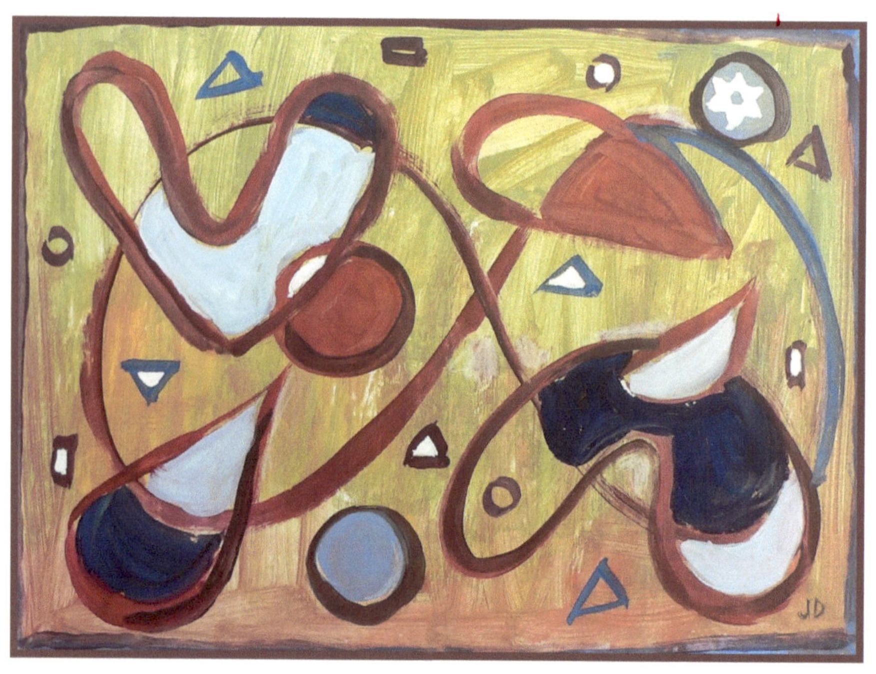

Hearts Floating

Acrylic on paper, 27 x 39 cm, 2010

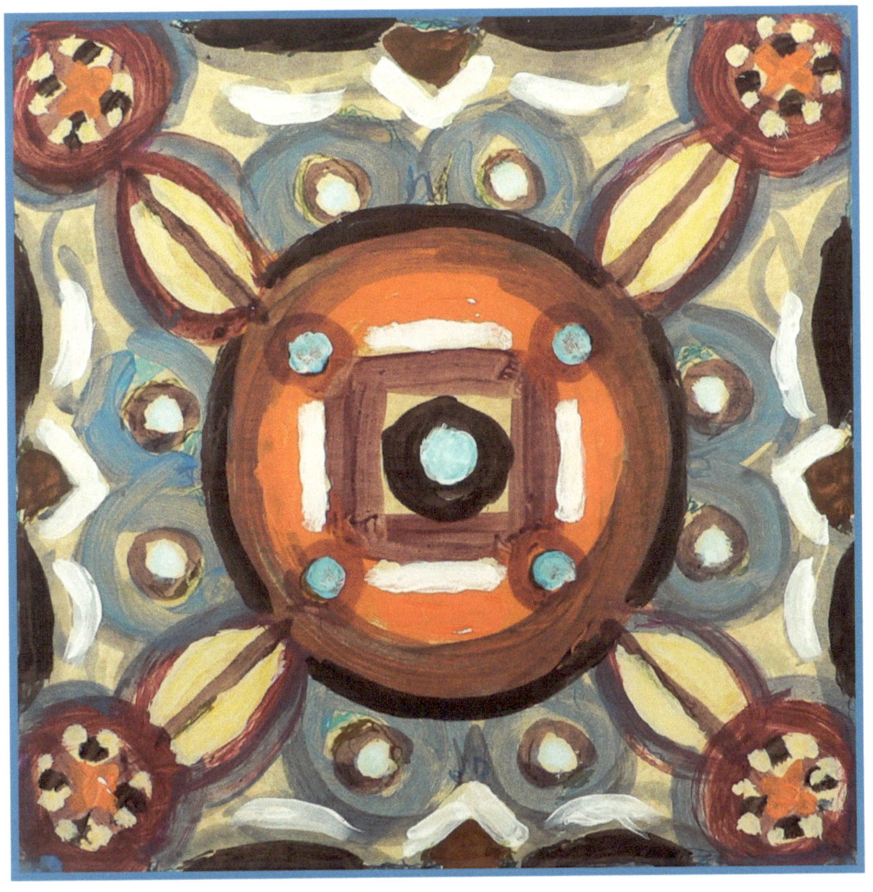

Circle Glowing

Acrylic on paper, 27 x 27 cm, 2008

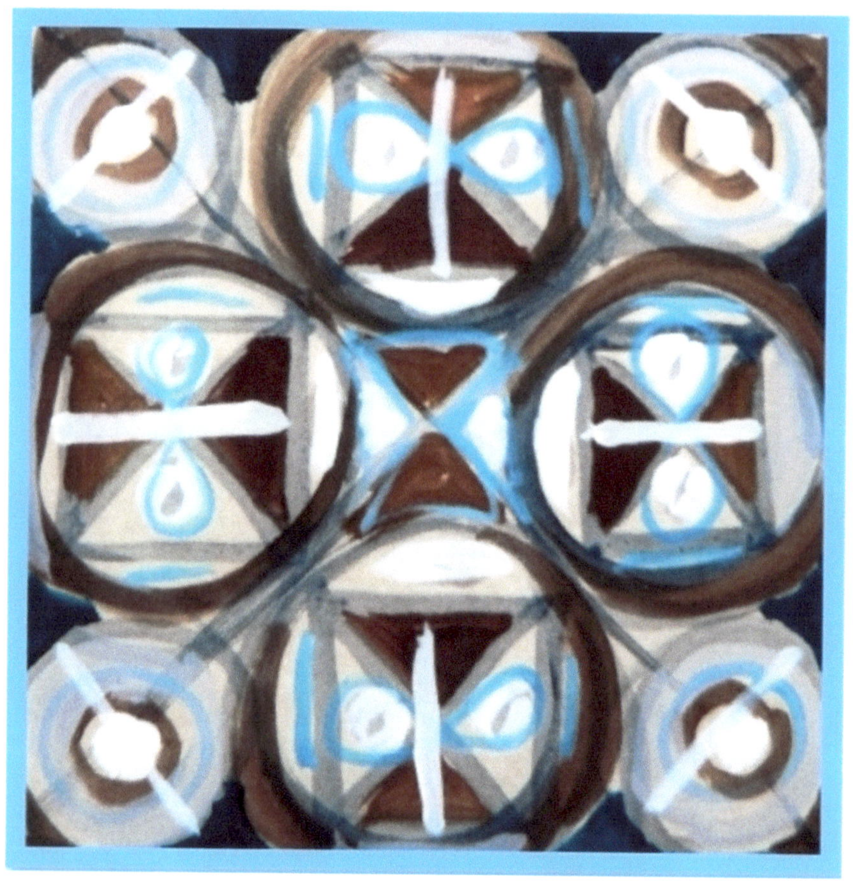

Memory

Acrylic on paper, 28 x 28 cm, 2007

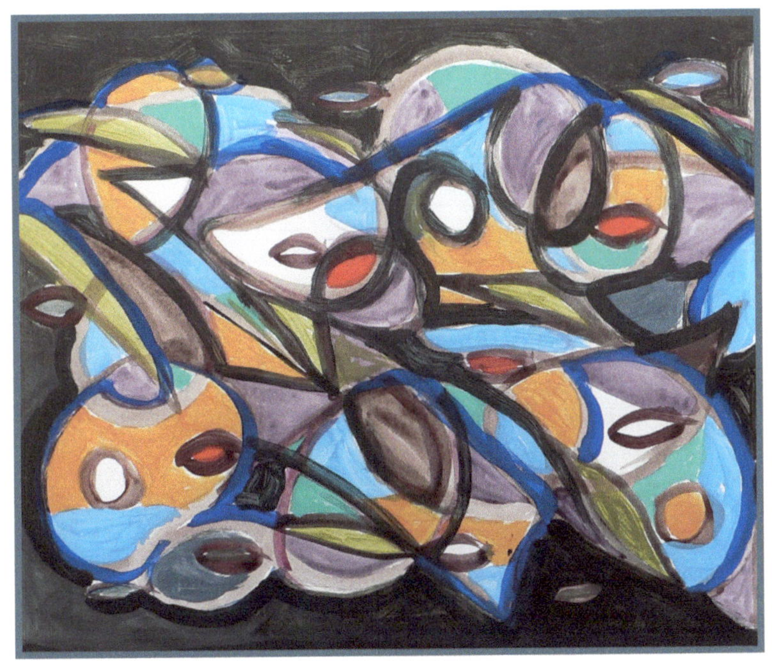

Memories

Acrylic on paper, 37 x 29 cm, 2007

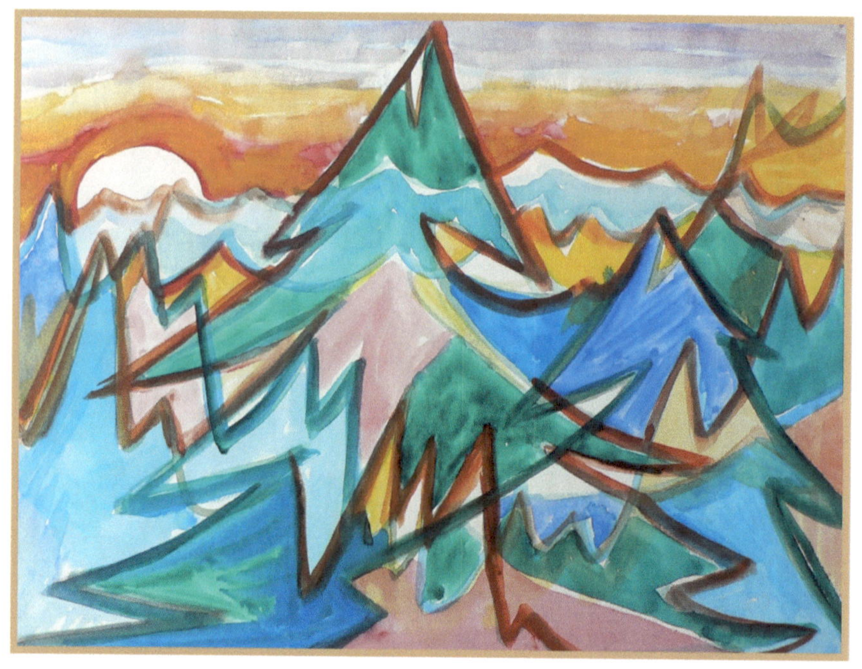

Rising Sun

Watercolour on paper, 27 x 36 cm, 2005

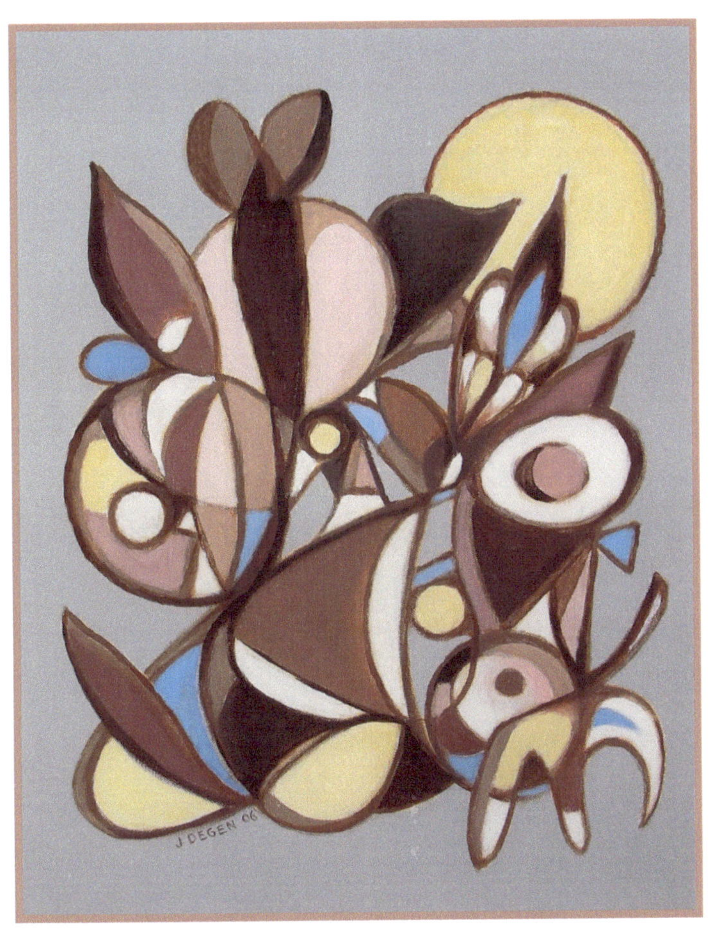

Soliloquy

Oil on canvas, 60 x 50 cm, 2006

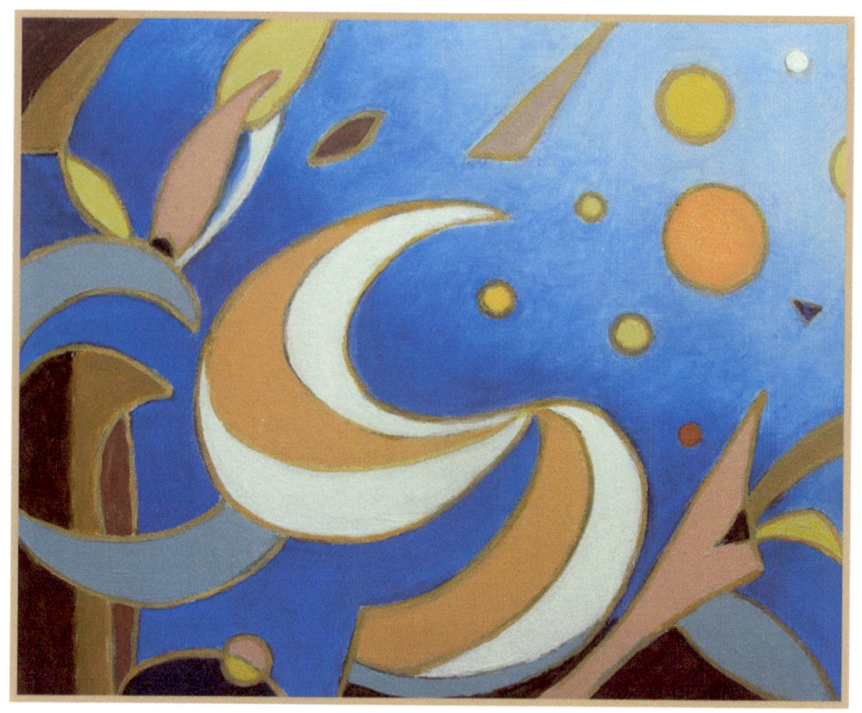

Field of View

Acrylic on canvas, 40 x 50 cm, 2012

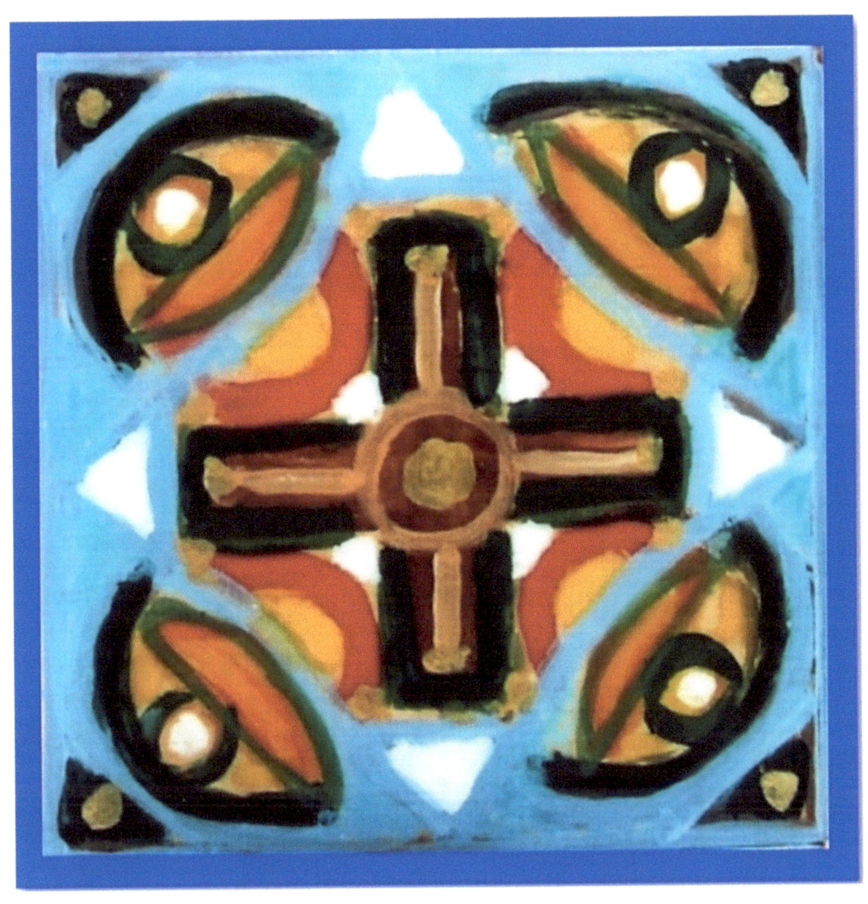

Peace

Acrylic on paper, 28 x 28 cm, 2007

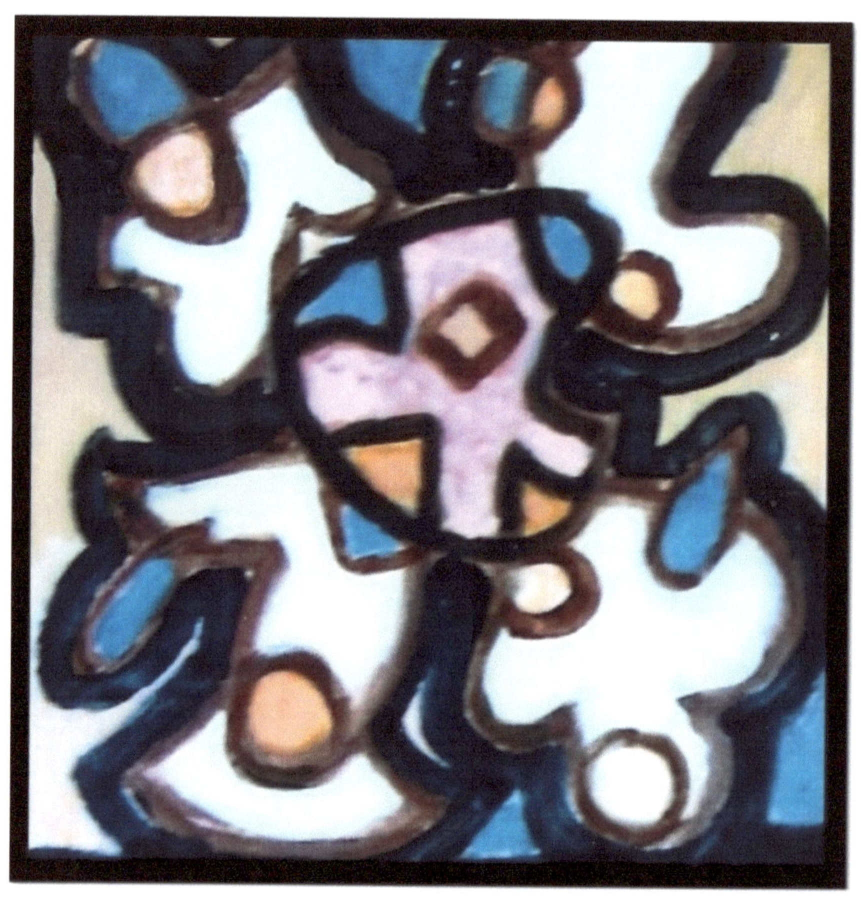

Company

Acrylic on paper, 27 x 27 cm, 2007

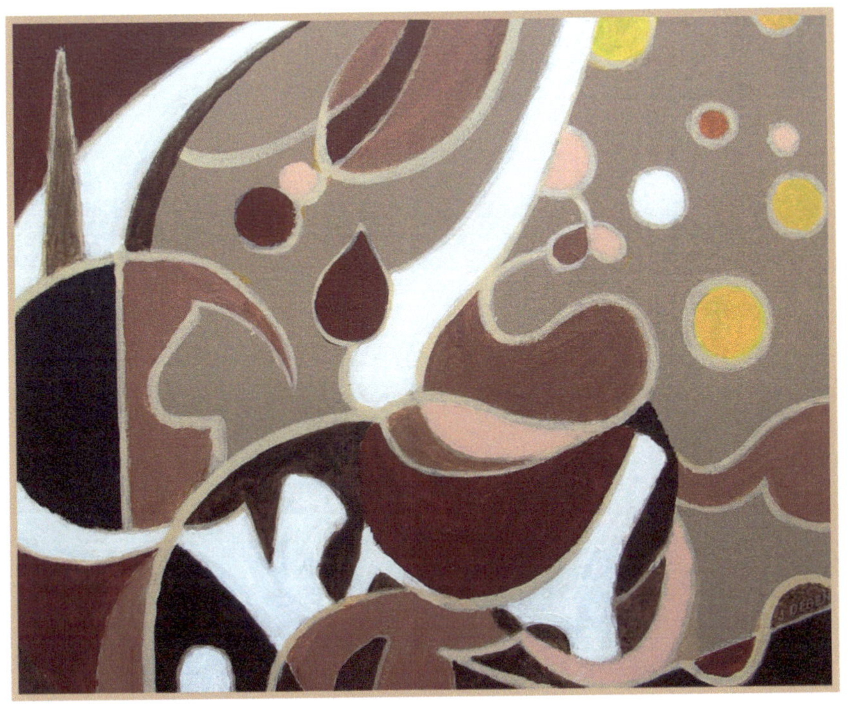

Activity

Acrylic on canvas, 40 x 50 cm, 2012

*Life beats down and crushes the soul
and art reminds you that you have one.*
~ Stella Adler

The artist must train not only his eye but also his soul.
~ Wassily Kandinsky

Colour is a power which directly influences the soul.
~ Wassily Kandinsky

*Every artist dips his brush in his own soul, and paints his
own nature into his pictures.*
~ Henry Ward Beecher

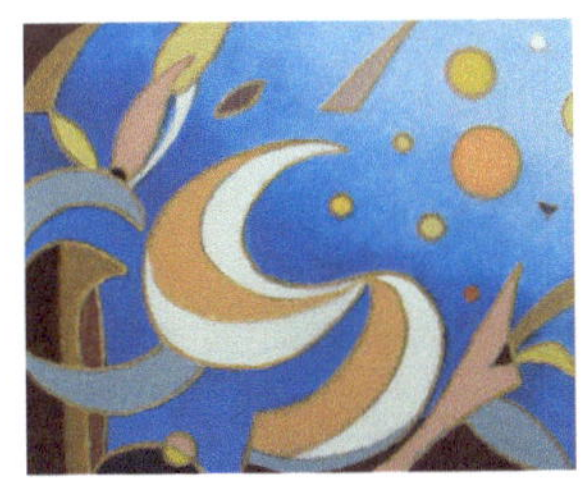

Meditation

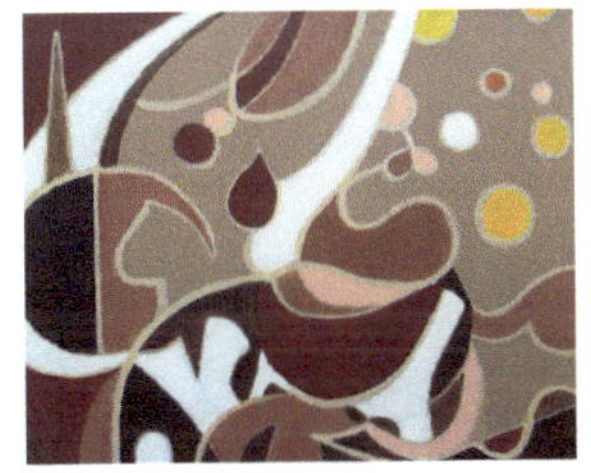

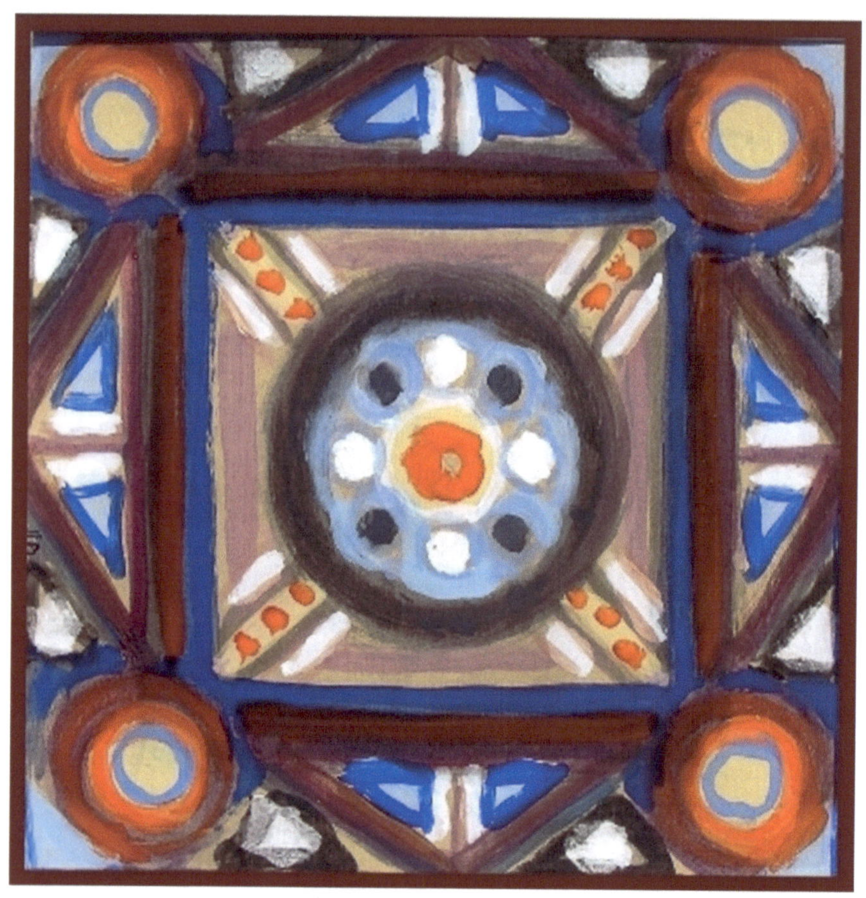

Silence

Acrylic on paper 28 x 28 cm, 2010

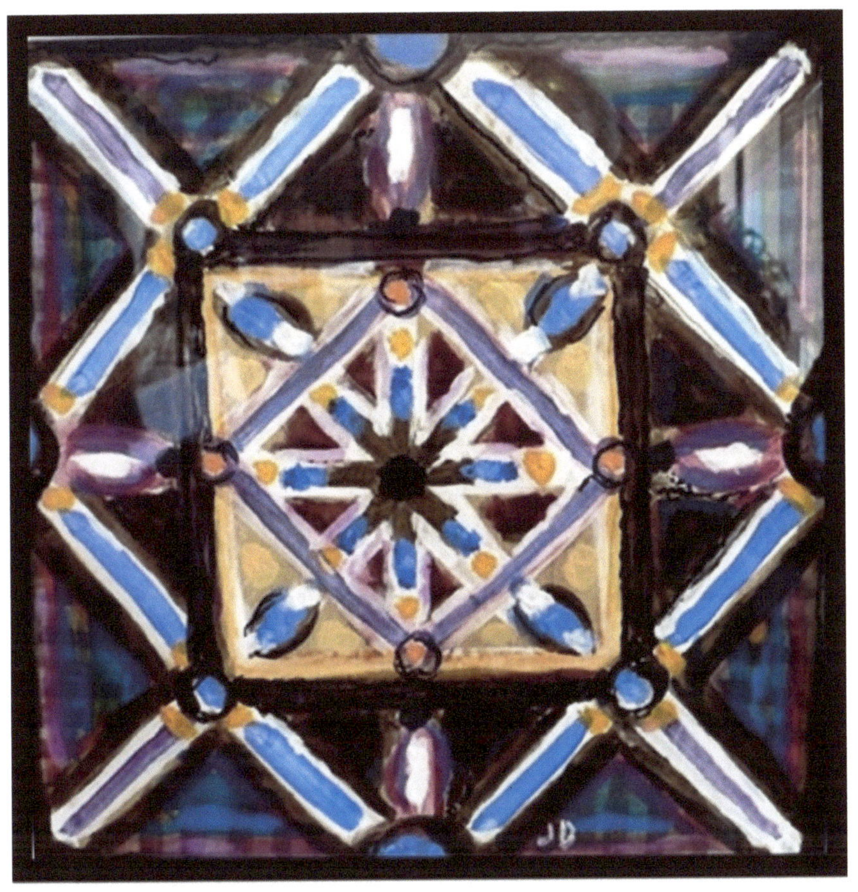

Contemplation

Acrylic on paper 28 x 28 cm, 2010

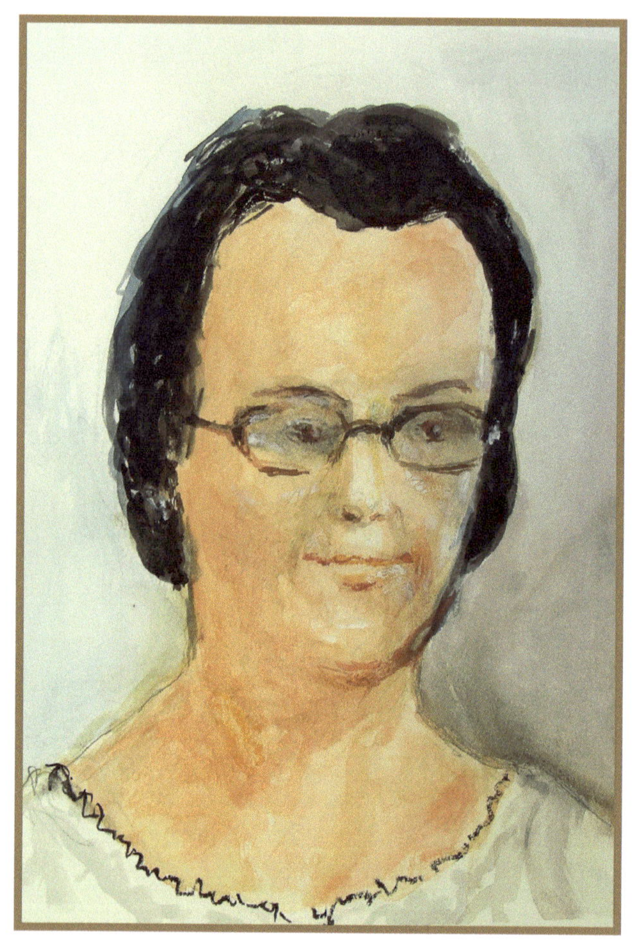

Concentration

Gouache on paper, 37 x 28 cm, 2009

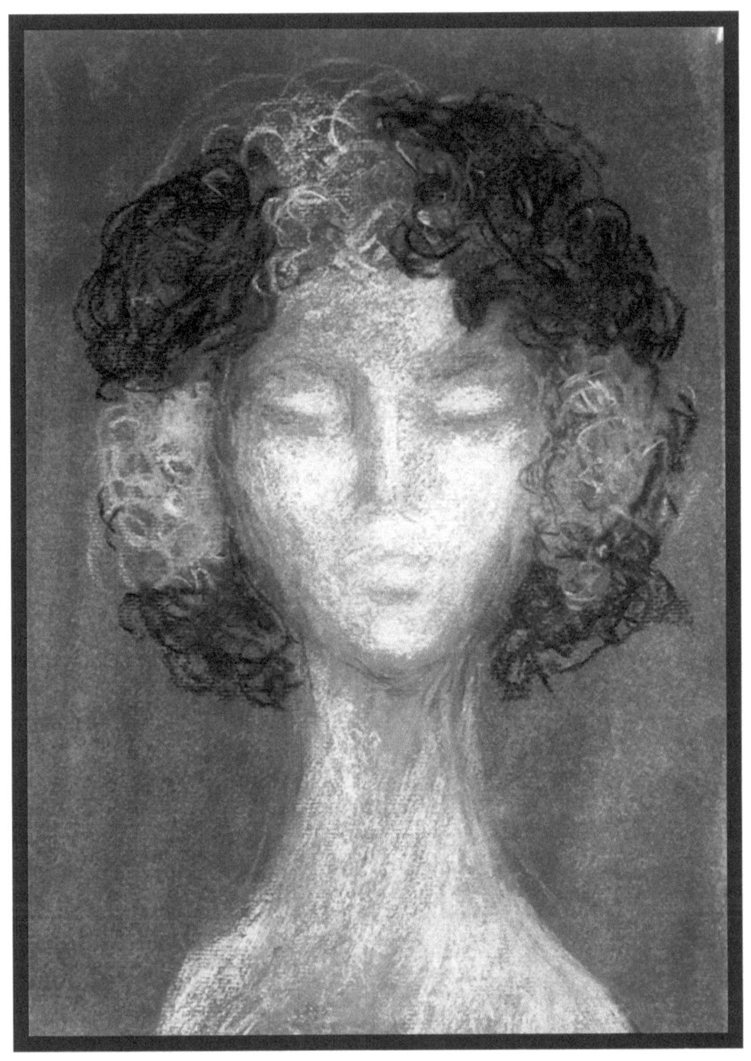

Meditating

Pastel on paper, 37 x 28 cm, 2010

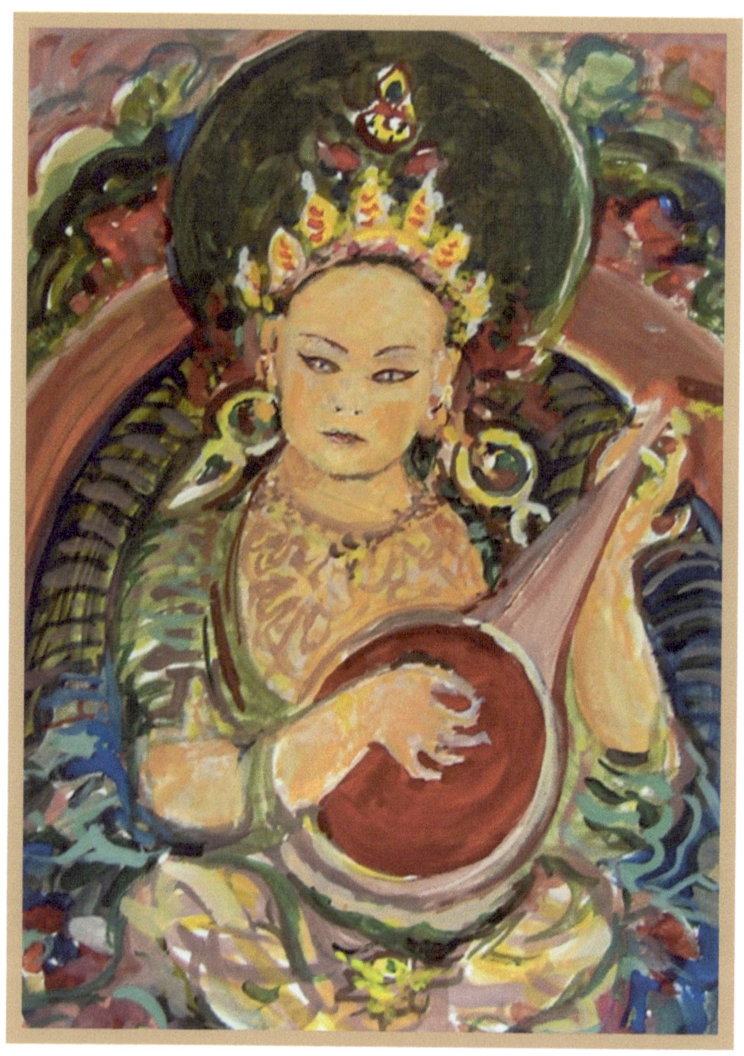

In the Temple

Gouache on paper, 37 x 28 cm, 2004

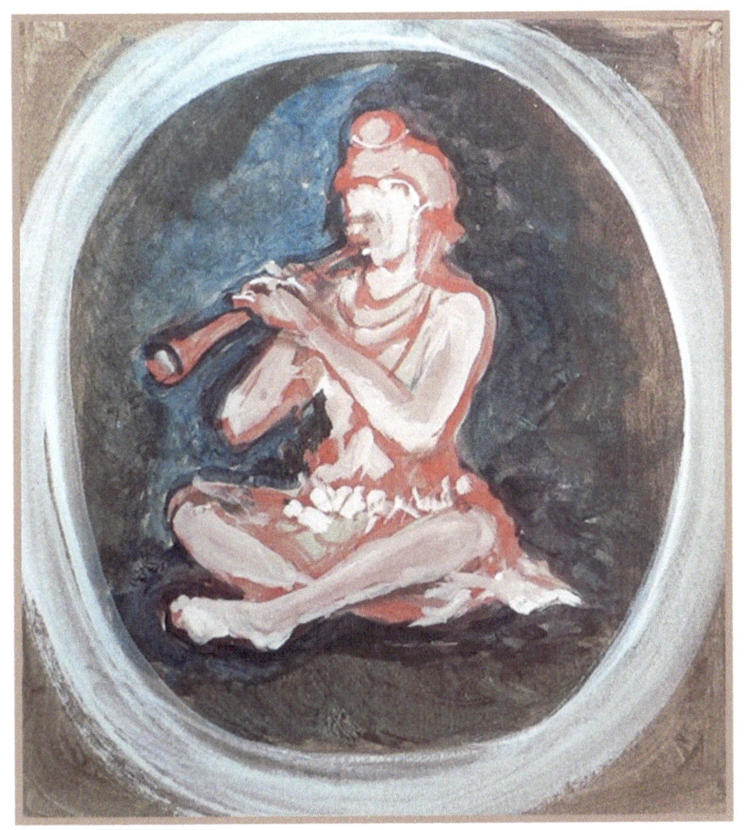

Meditation in Music

Acrylic on paper, 27 x 24 cm, 2003

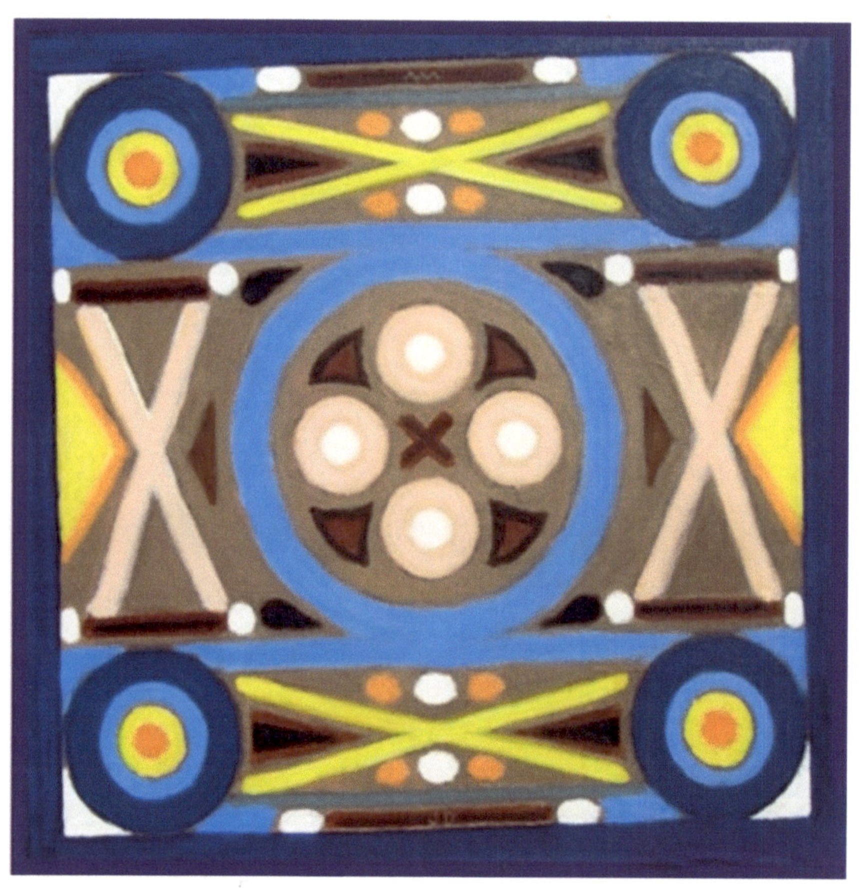

Meditation

Acrylic on paper, 60 x 60 cm, 2007

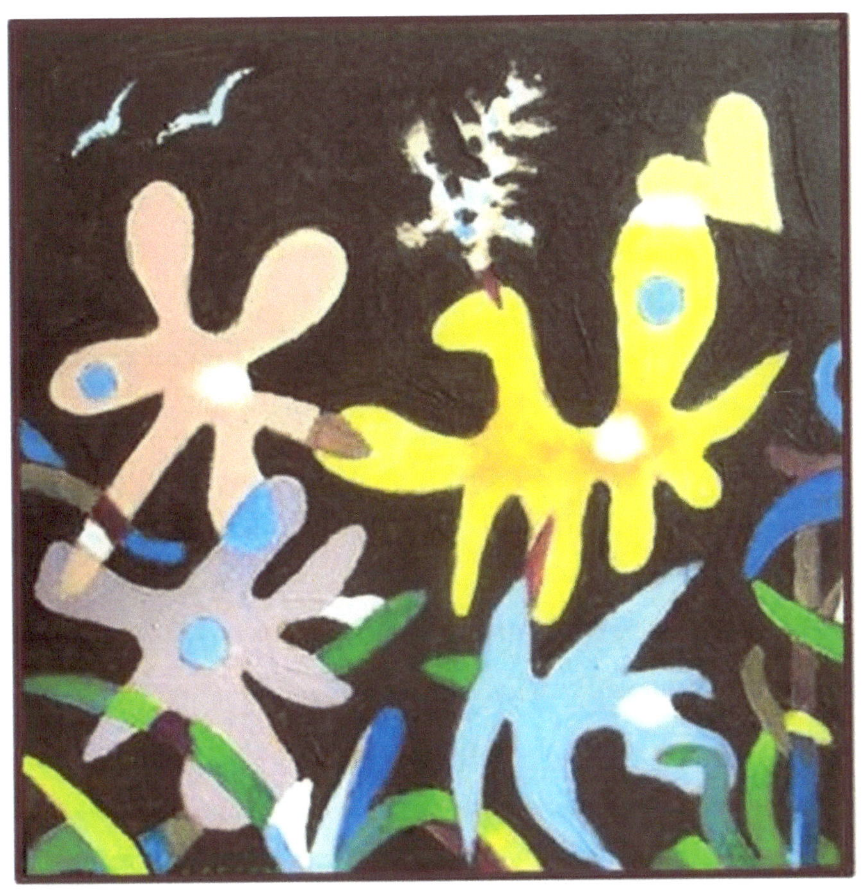

Sound of Colours

Acrylic on canvas, 60 x 60 cm, 2010

Art is something about the spirit.
~ Shary Boyle

Abstraction, among other things,
provides a separation from the daily, visible world,
with all its chaos and violence,
and attempts to recapture a sense of the numinous
through a regard for pure color, pure shape, pure form.
~ Chris Morrison

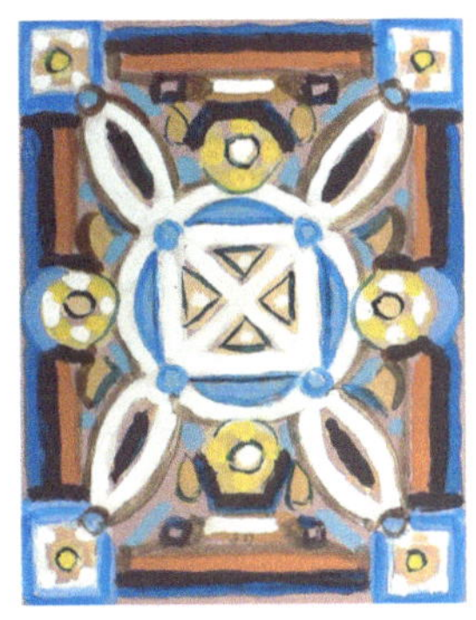

Mandalas

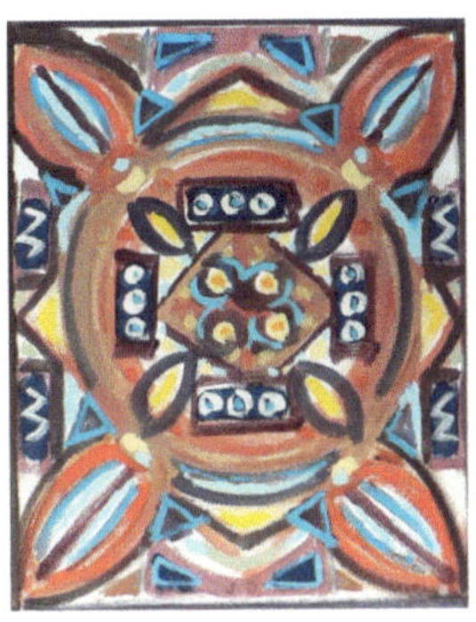

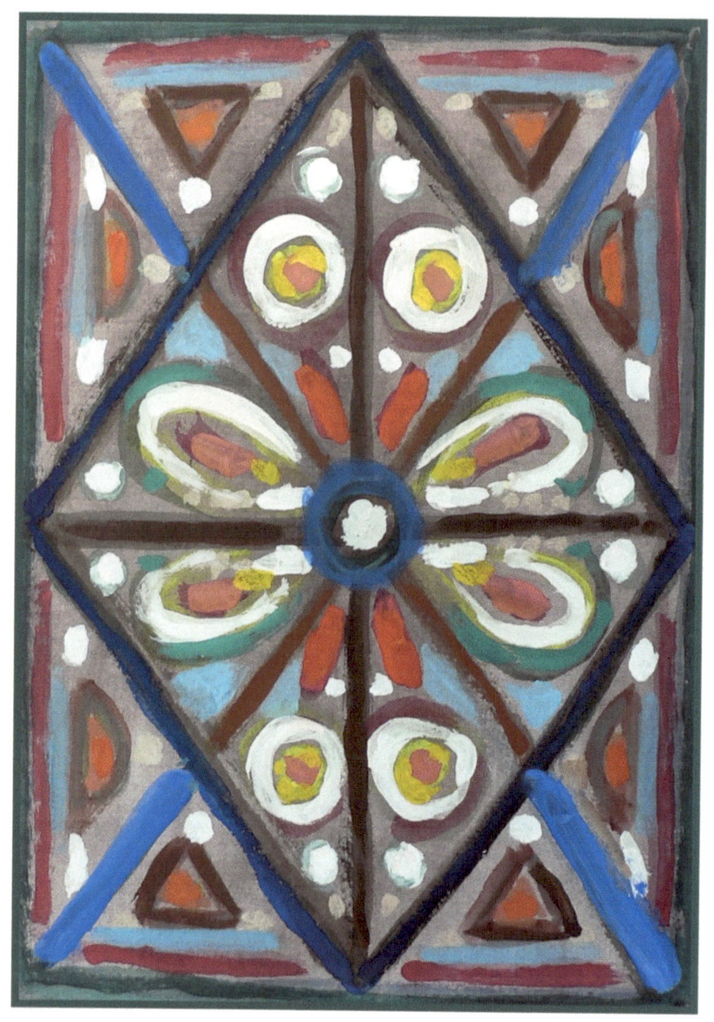

Mandala

Acrylic on paper, 37 x 27 cm, 2011

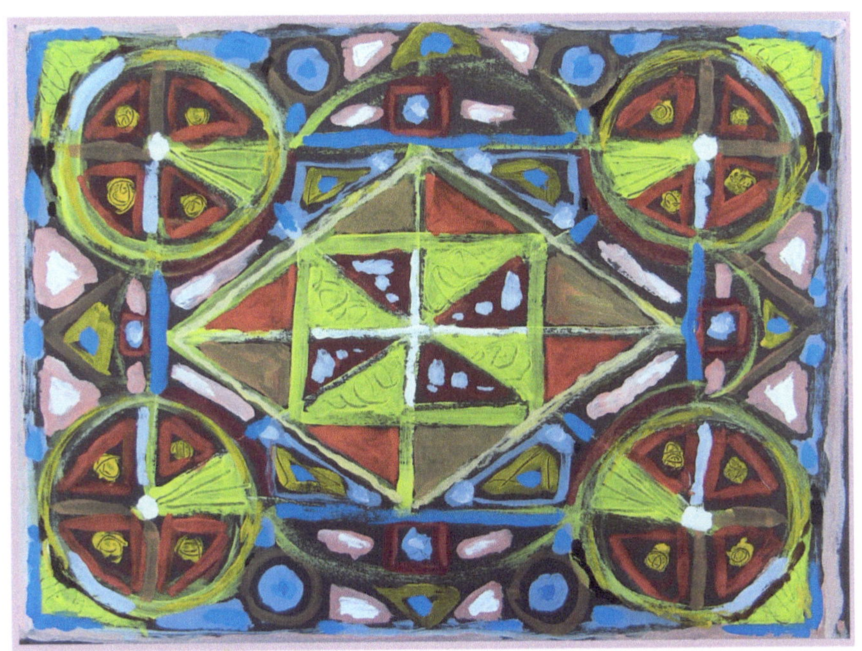

Mood of Mandala

Acrylic on paper, 70 x 42 cm, 2005

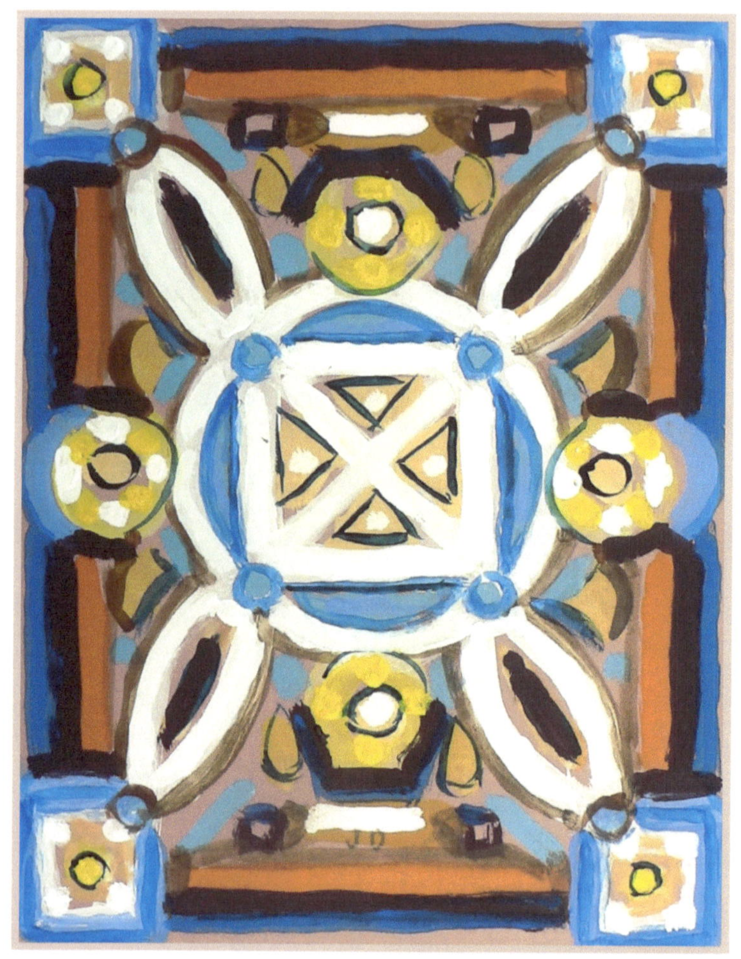

Mandala Inspiration

Acrylic on board, 36 x 28 cm, 2011

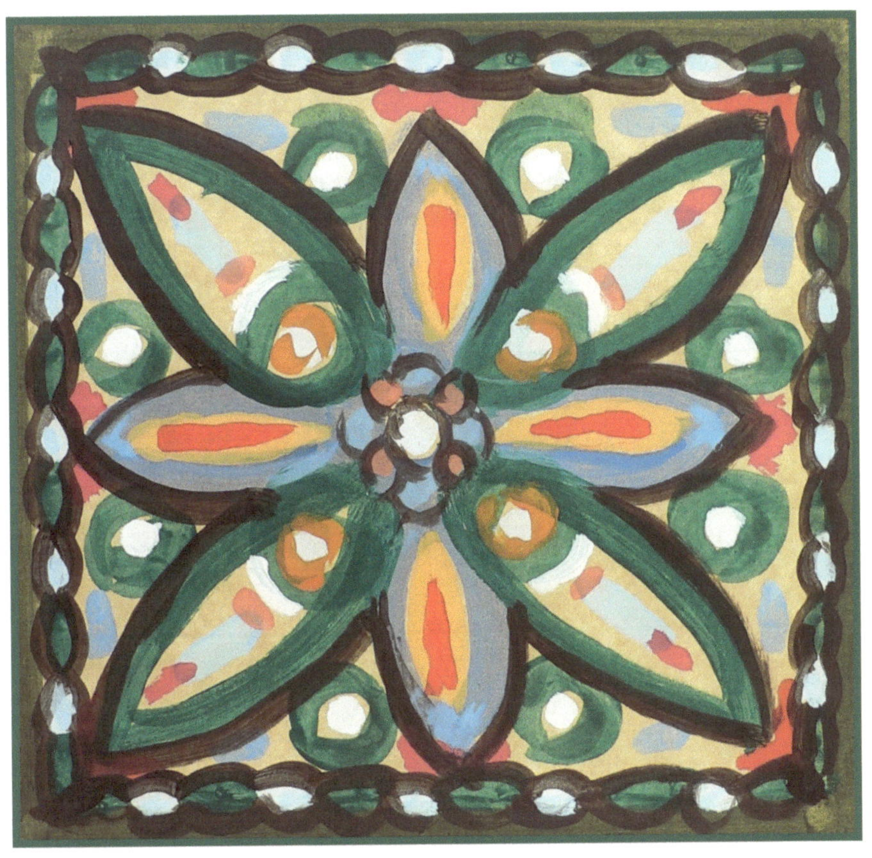

Garden Mandala

Acrylic on paper, 26 x 28 cm, 2007

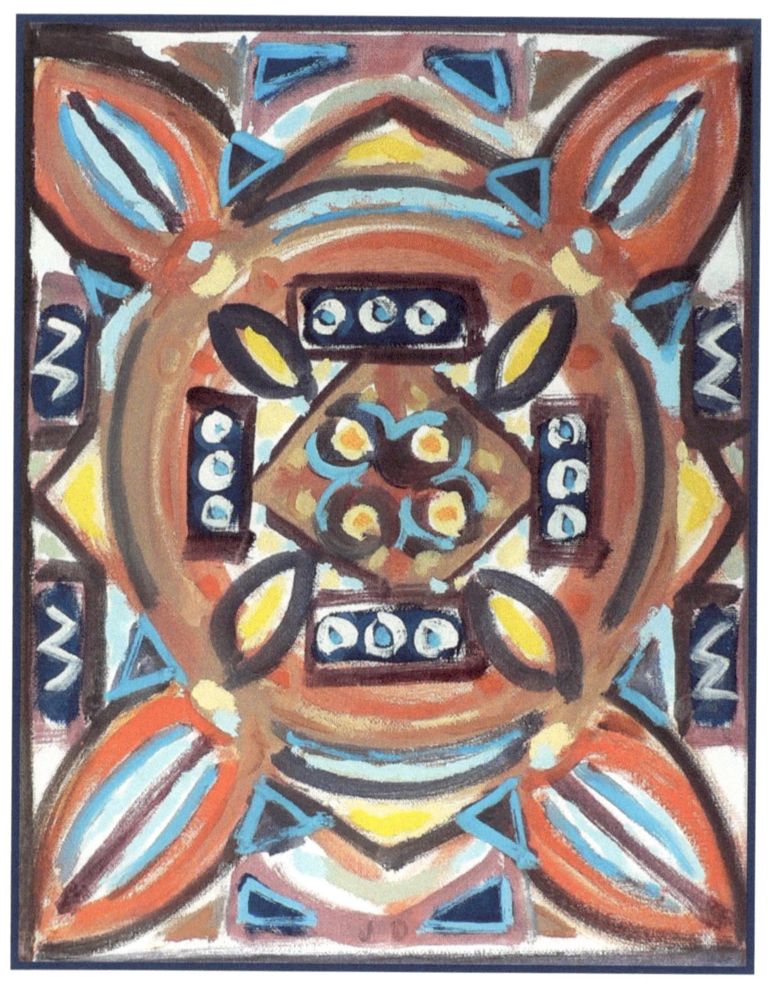

Red Mandala

Oil on canvas, 37 x 29 cm, 2005

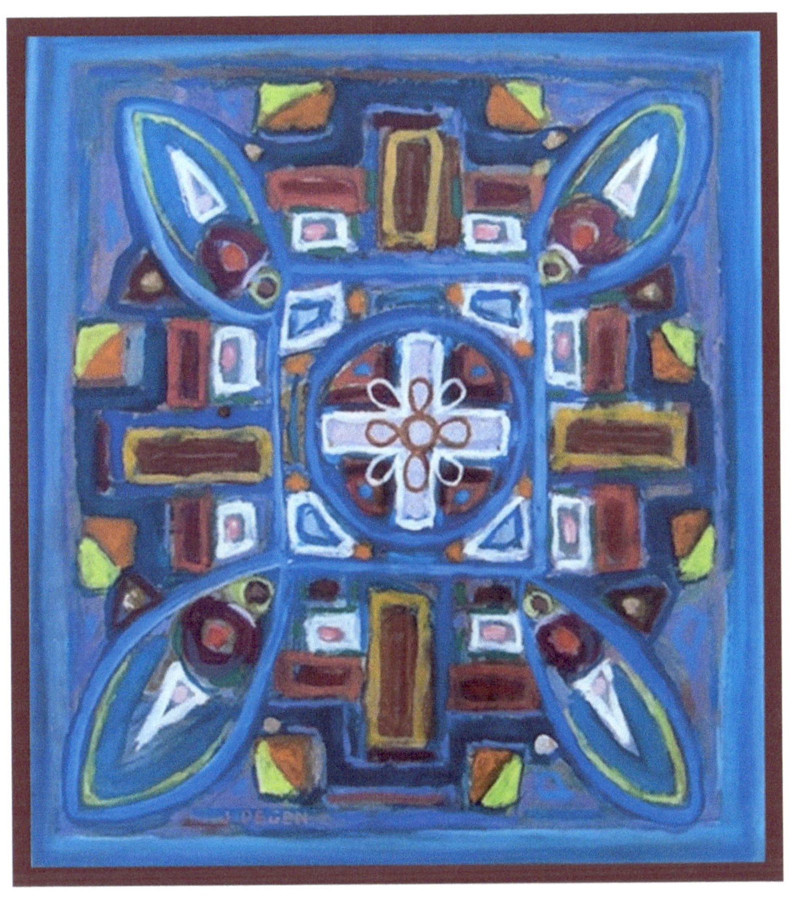

Mandala in Blue

Oil on board, 50 x 45 cm, 1997

The artist must have something to say,
for mastery over form is not his goal
but rather the adapting of form to its inner meaning.
~ Wassily Kandinsky

The true work of art is born from the artist:
a mysterious, enigmatic, and mystical creation.
It detaches itself from him, it acquires an autonomous
life, becomes a personality, an independent subject,
animated with a spiritual breath,
the living subject of a real existence of being.
~ Wassily Kandinsky

Christian Symbolism

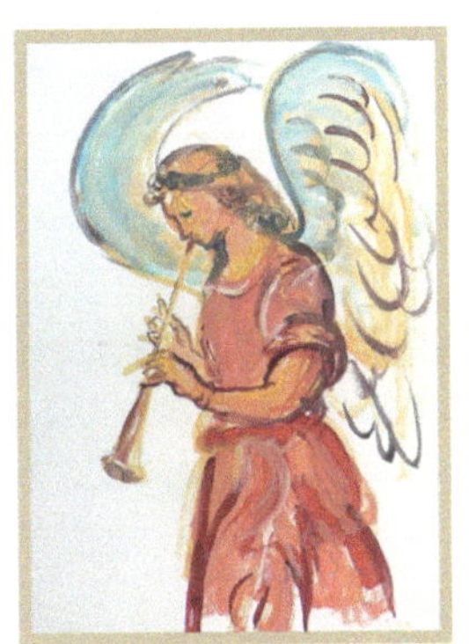

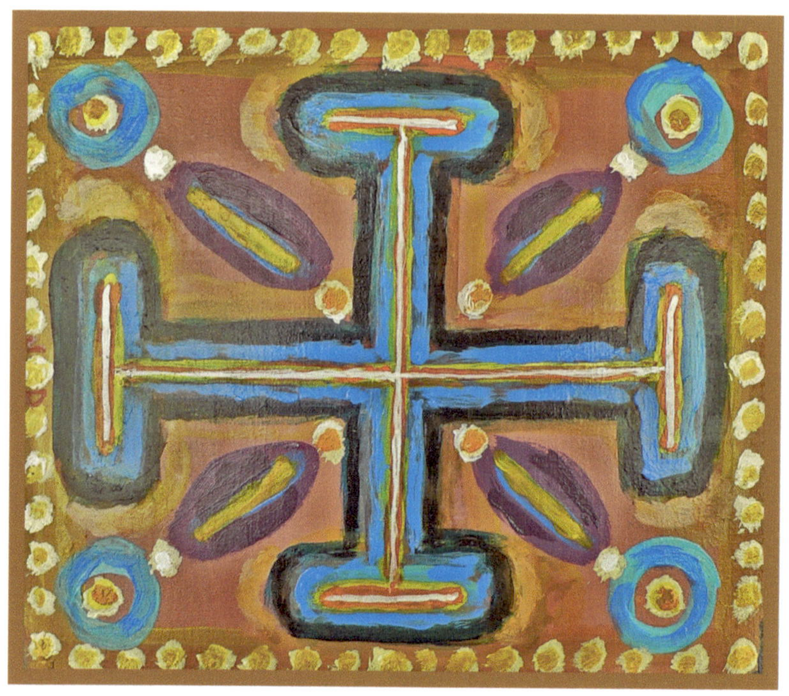

Symbol

Acrylic on board, 29 x 25 cm, 2012

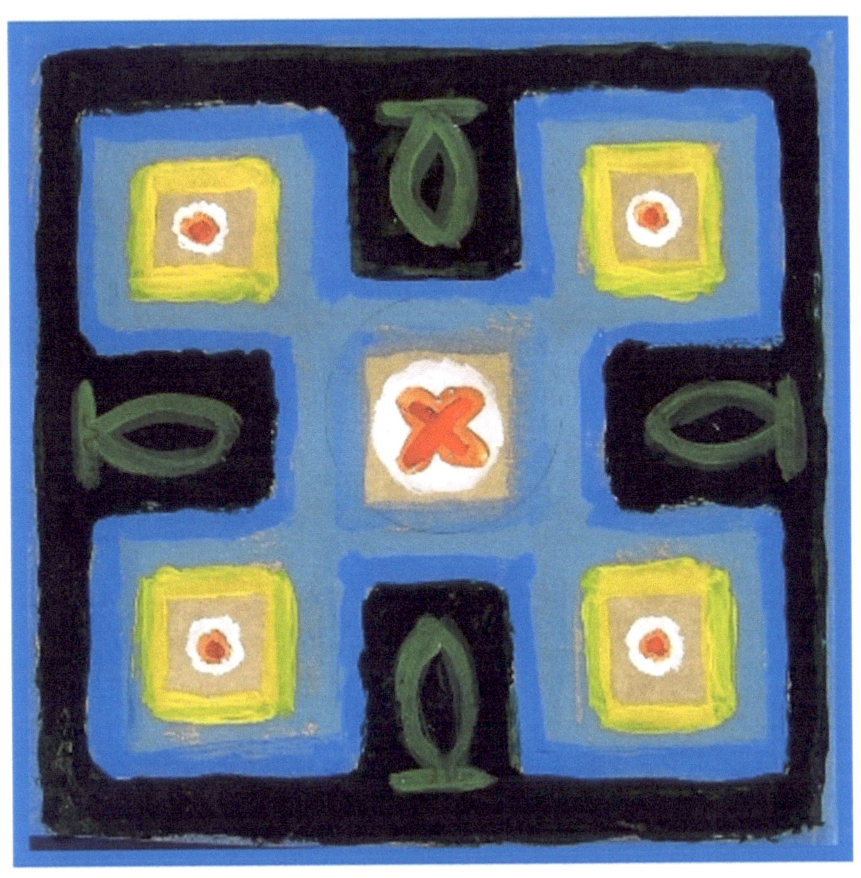

Blue Cross

Acrylic on paper, 28 x 28 cm, 2010

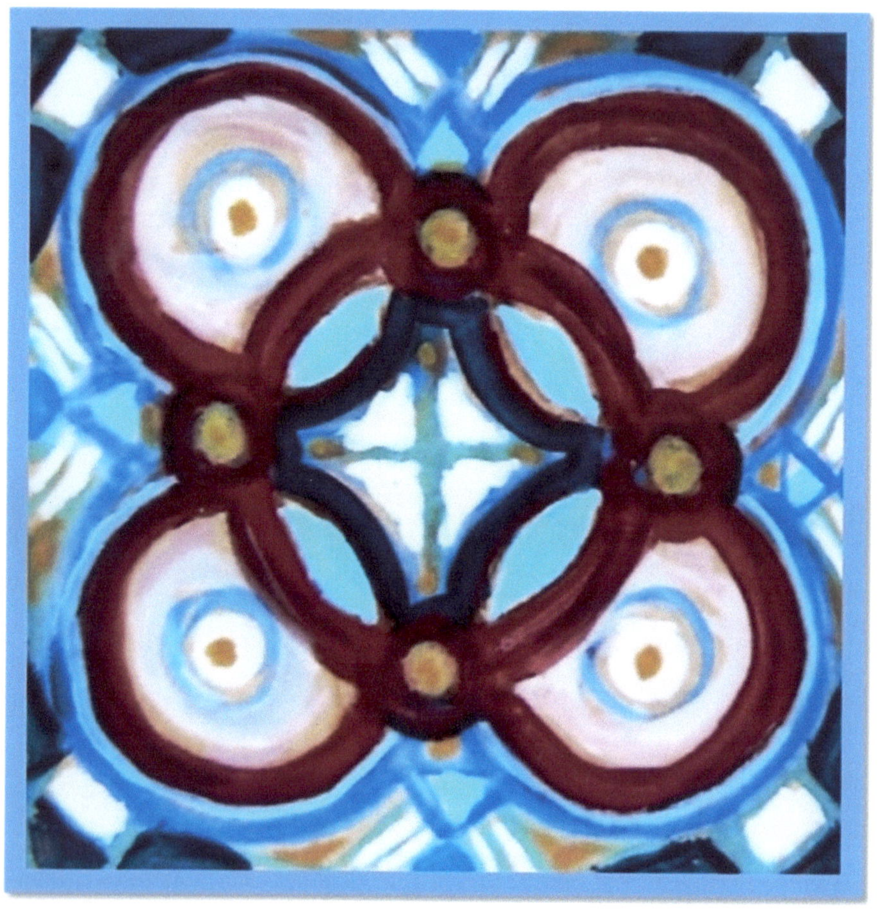

Basilica

Acrylic on paper, 28 x 28 cm, 2007

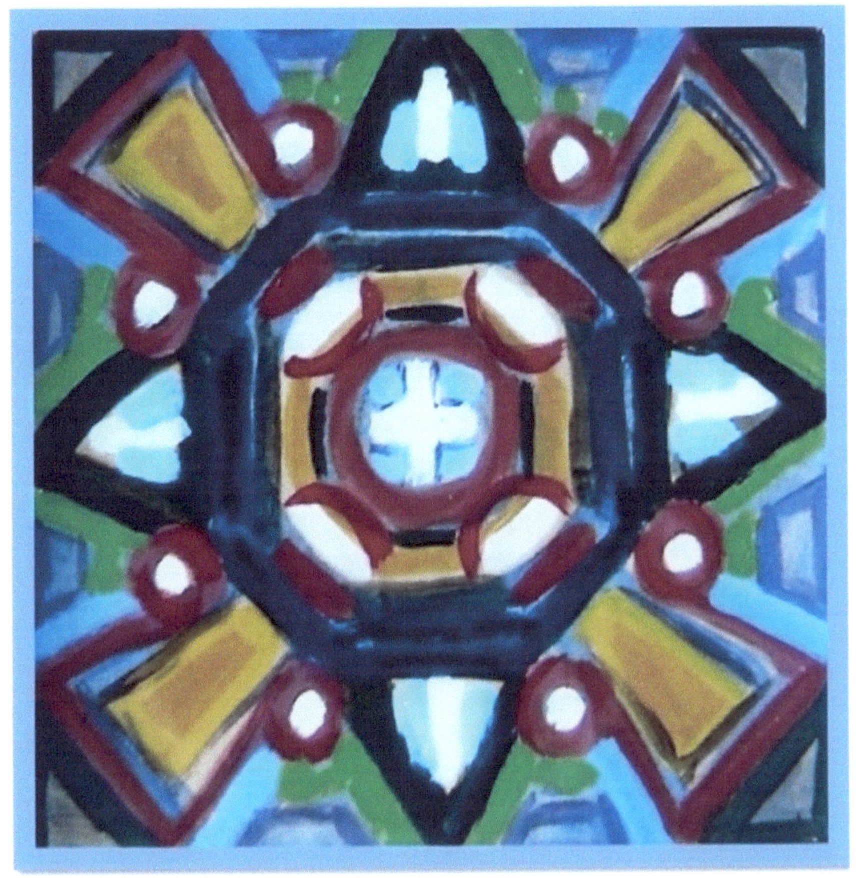

Basilica Dome

Acrylic on paper, 28 x 28 cm, 2005

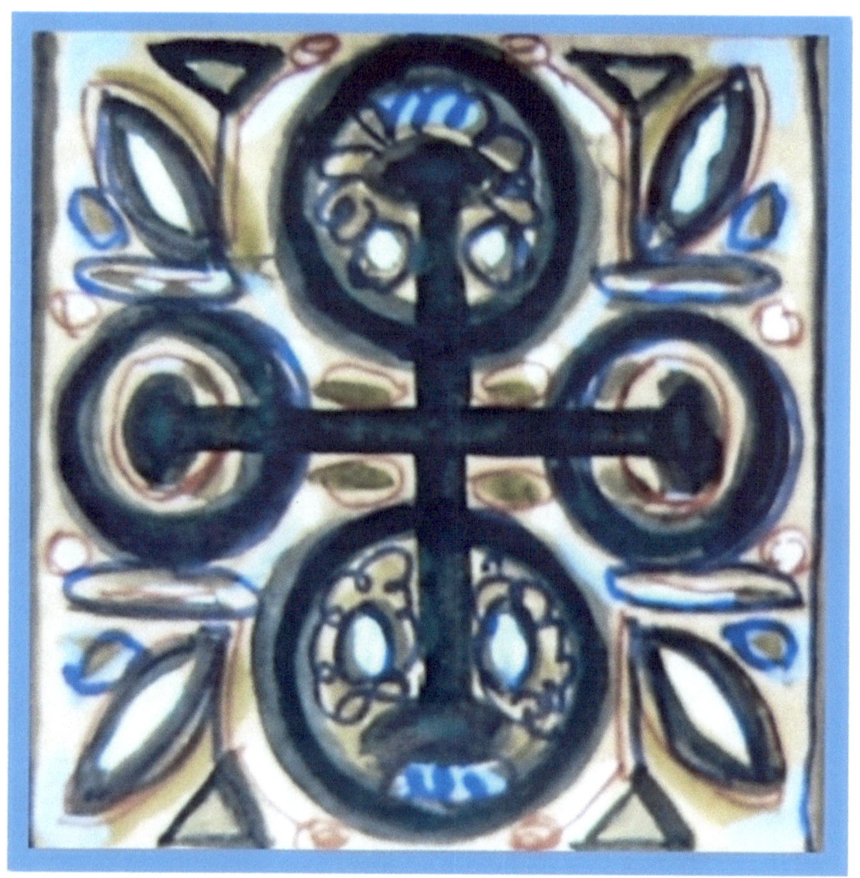

Byzantium

Acrylic on paper, 27 x 27 cm, 2006

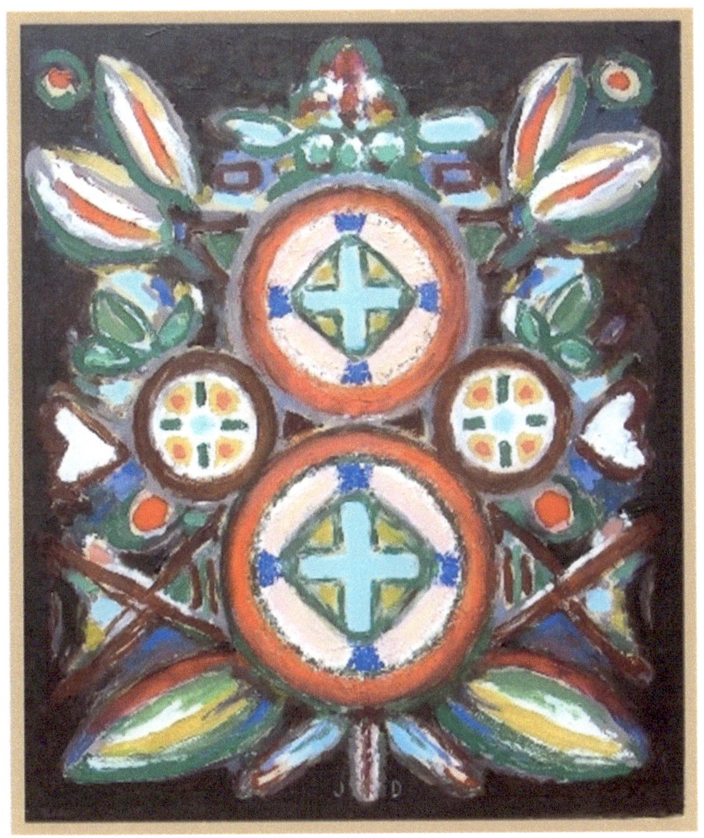

Christian Memories

Oil on board, 60 x 50 cm, 2009

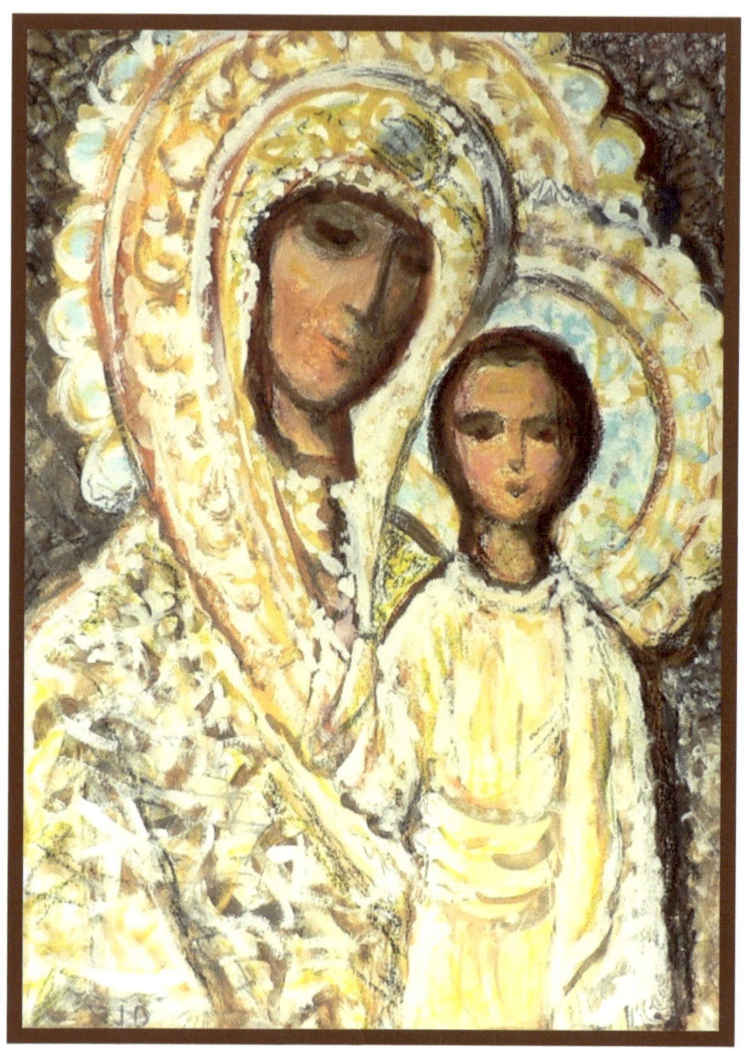

Madonna

Oil and charcoal on canvas, 39 x 28 cm, 2007

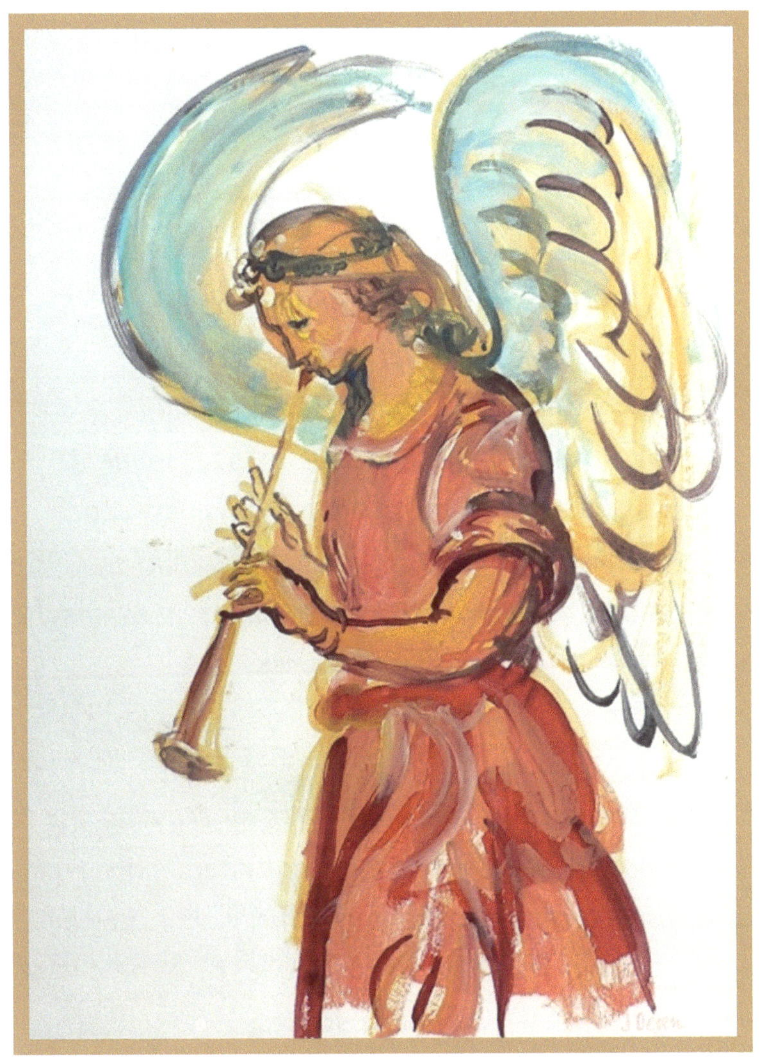

Angel Playing

Acrylic on paper, 37 x 27 cm, 2002

*The work of art is born of the artist
in a mysterious and secret way.
From him it gains life and being.
Nor is its existence casual or inconsequent,
but it has a definite and purposeful strength,
alike in its material and spiritual life.
It exists and has power to create spiritual atmosphere.*
~ Wassily Kandinsky

*First, one seeks to become an artist by training the hand.
Then one finds it is the eye that needs improving.
Later one learns it is the mind that wants developing,
only to find that the ultimate quest of the artist
is in the spirit.*
~ Larry Brullo

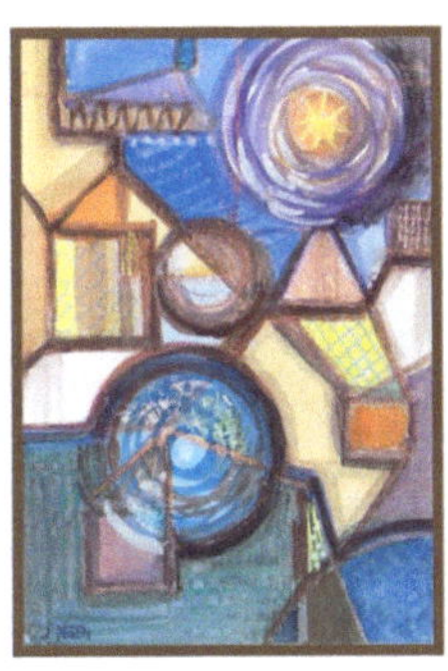

Celebration

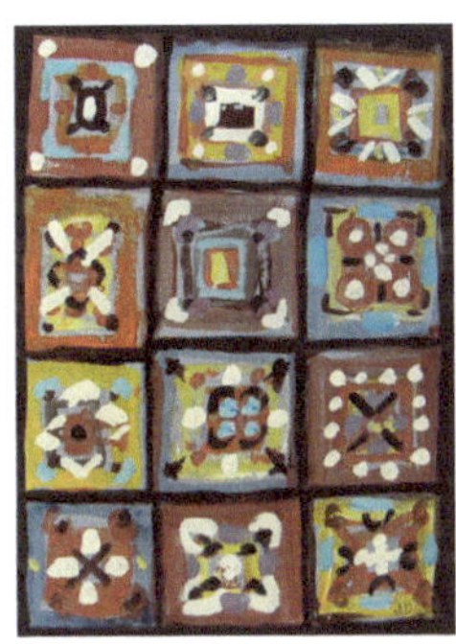

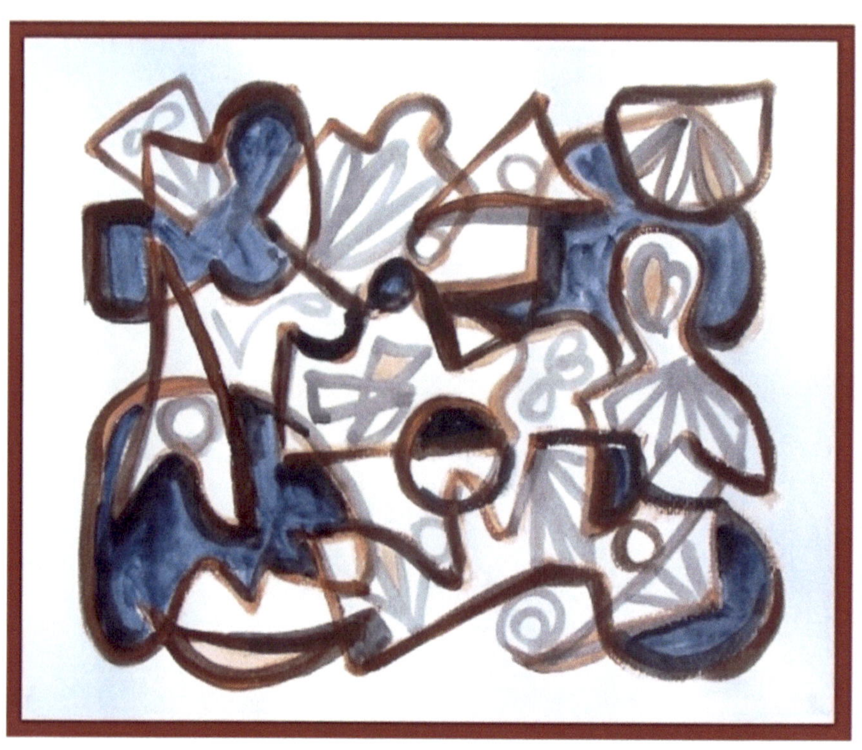

Silent Celebration

Acrylic on paper, 28 x 36 cm, 2009

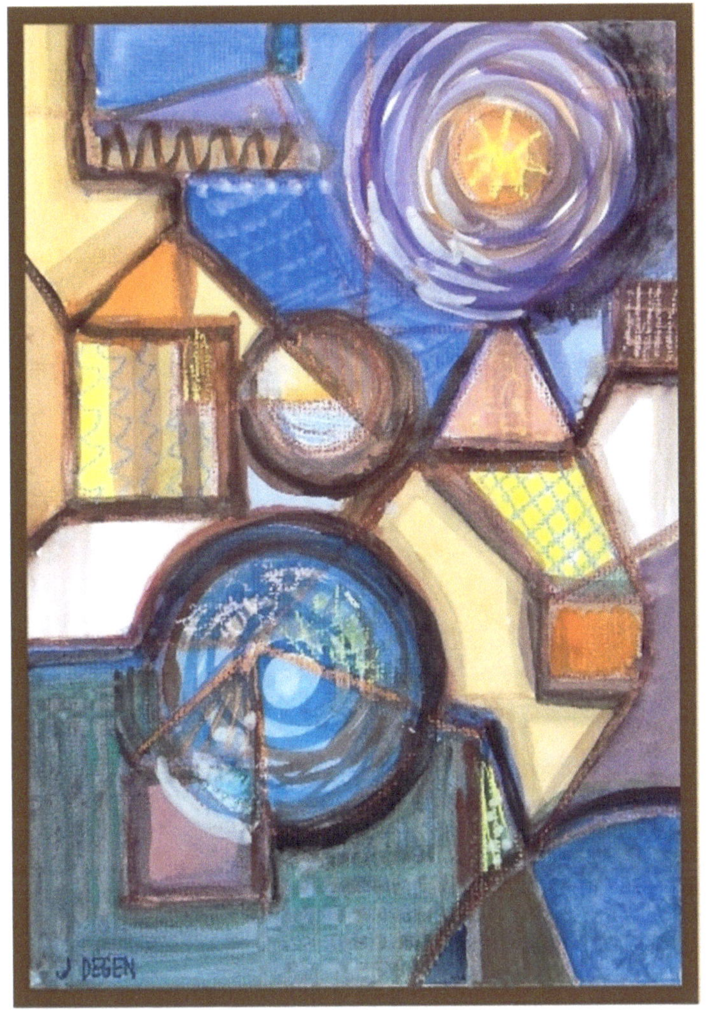

The Feast

Acrylic on board, 43.5 x 36 cm, 2009

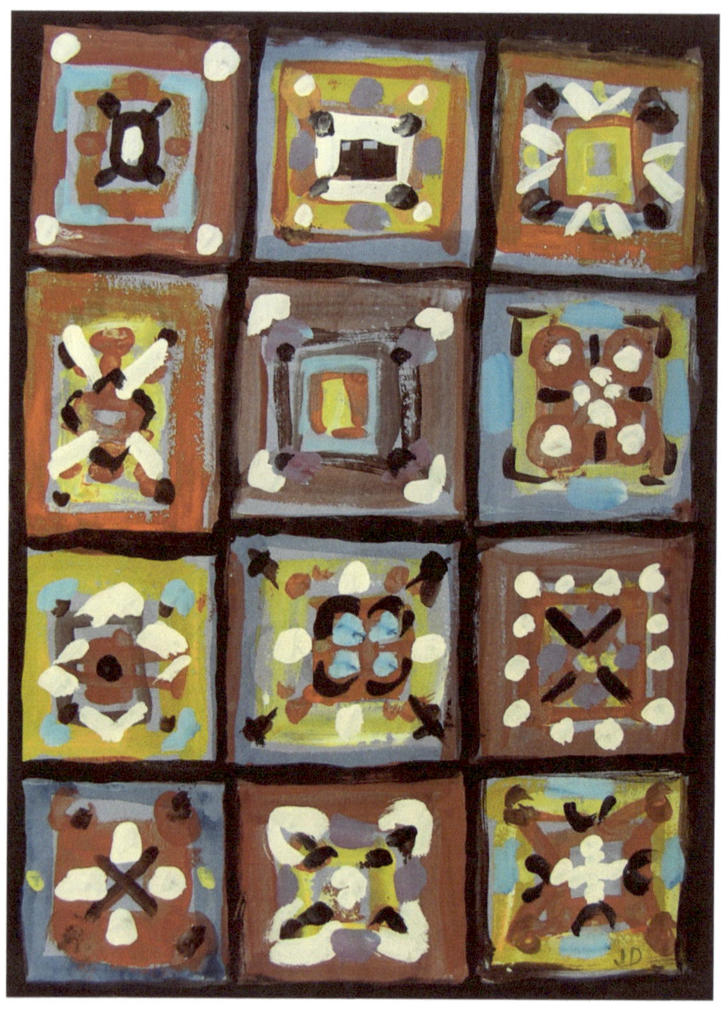

The Great Feast

Acrylic on paper, 36 x 27 cm, 2001

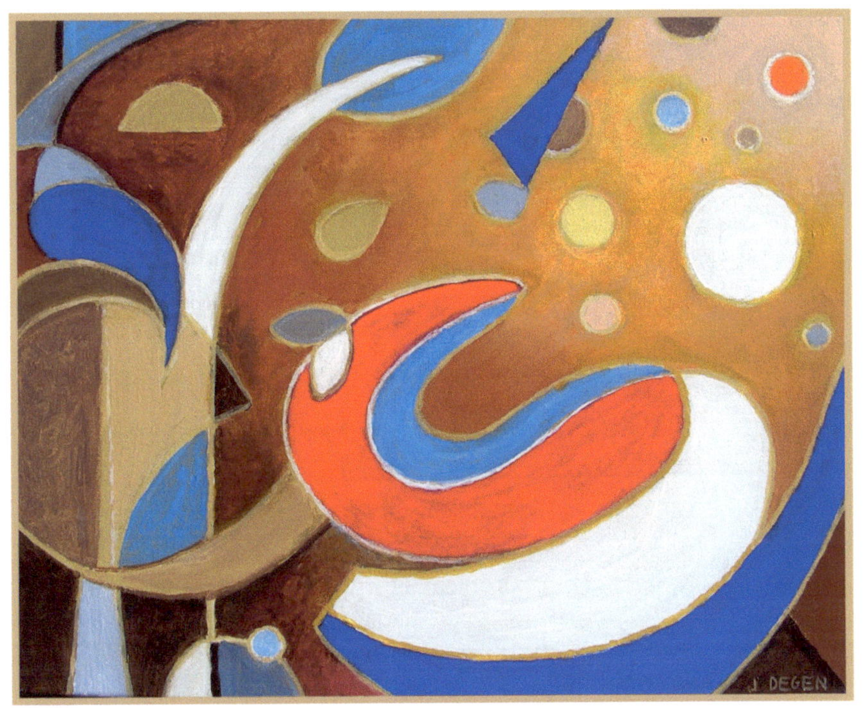

Euphoria

Acrylic on canvas, 40 x 50 cm, 2012

MORE ABOUT JINDRICH'S BOOKS

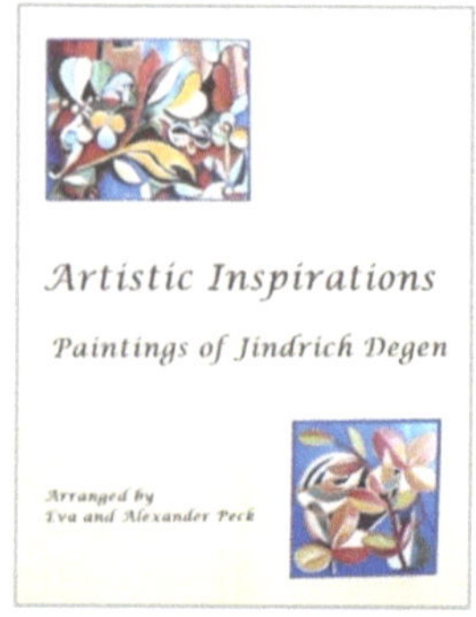

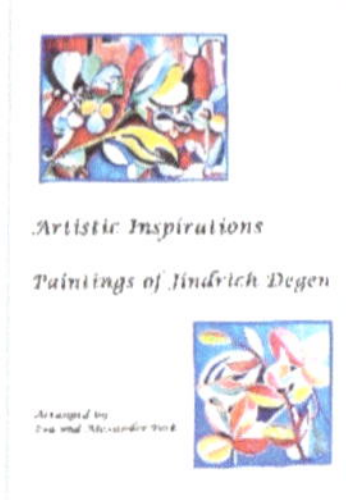

Artistic Inspirations: Paintings of Jindrich Degen features 200 of Jindrich (Henry) Degen's paintings. A range of diverse subjects is presented in both realistic and abstract art. The art works, produced in various media, are organized under twelve themes. This book is available in two editions – large (deluxe) and small (budget).

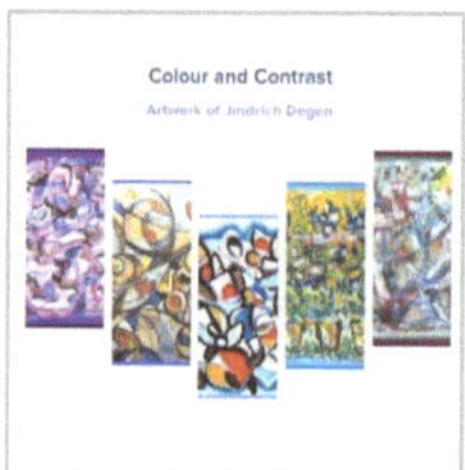

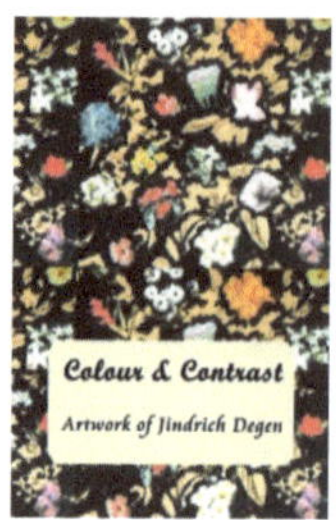

Colour and Contrast: Artwork of Jindrich Degen features the same works as *Artistic Inspirations*. It however showcases each piece of art on a separate page. Also available in a budget edition.

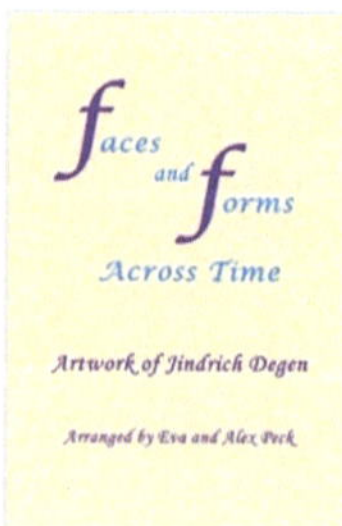

Faces and Forms Across Time is a selection of drawings and paintings by Jindrich (Henry) Degen featuring real-life portraits; portraits drawn from photos or works of other artists; icons and symbols; wild and domestic animals; as well as products of Jindrich's imagination.

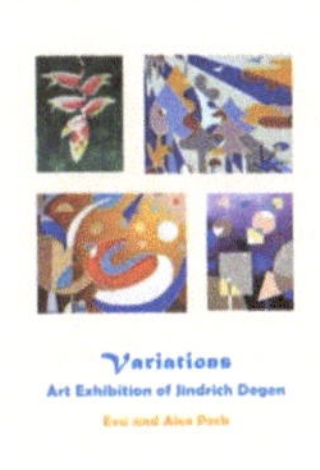

Variations documents an art exhibition of Jindrich Degen held in November 2013 at the Yurara Art Society gallery in Thornlands, Queensland. It takes readers on a journey through an art show from preparation to packing up.

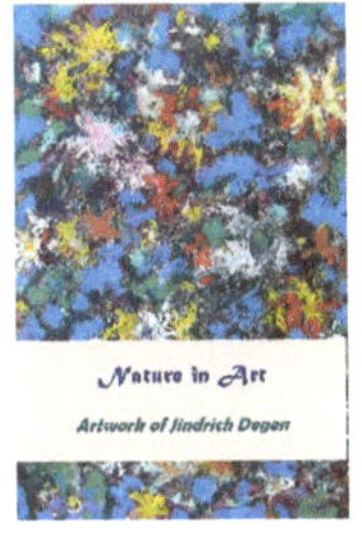

Nature in Art: Artwork of Jindrich Degen consists of paintings relating to themes of nature including land and sea; trees, leaves and flowers; and living creatures. A section entitled "Fantasy" features original works from Jindrich's imagination.

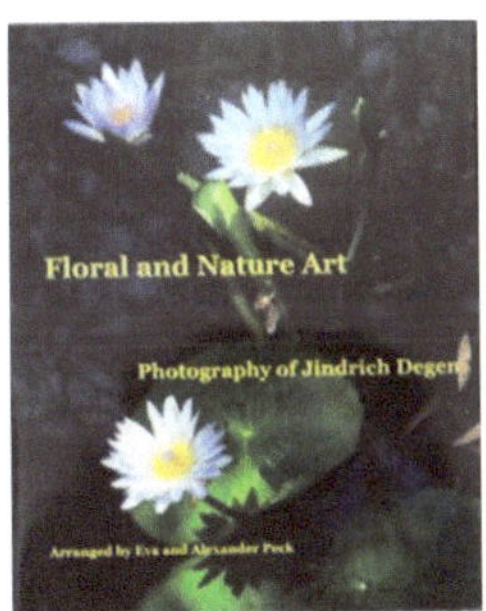

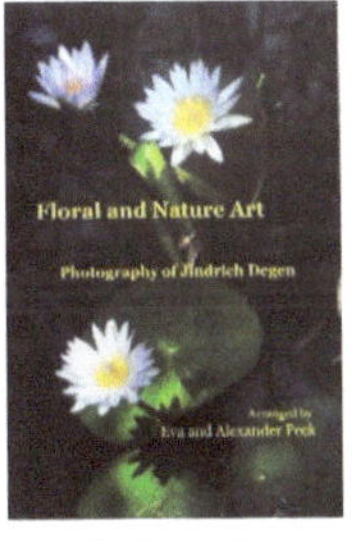

Floral and Nature Art: Photography of Jindrich Degen presents digital photography of Jindrich (Henry) Degen. The images of flowers and bushland settings, captured through the eyes of an artist, are arranged under the themes of floral art and nature art. Inspirational quotations on each page complement the photographic beauty. Available in a large (deluxe) and a small (budget) edition.

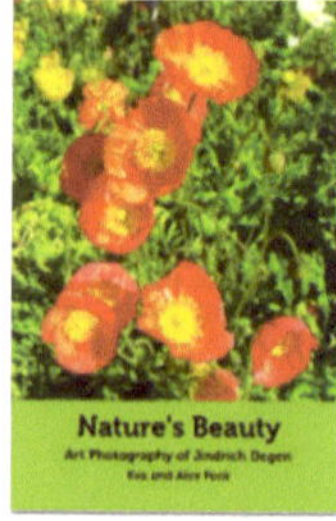

Nature's Beauty: Art Photography of Jindrich Degen features further digital photography of artist Jindrich (Henry) Degen. The images taken in natural settings of south-east Queensland reflect his imagination, giving many of his photos an artistic flair. The collection is arranged under ten themes and has complementing quotations on each page.

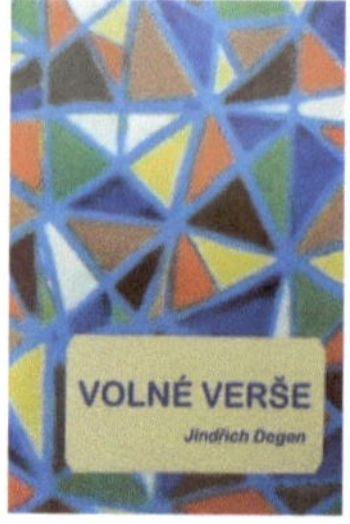

Volné verše (Free Verse) is a diverse collection of Czech verse and prose, often in a light-hearted form. Created over a decade, it was inspired by life's circumstances. It addresses current issues of science and technology, as well as capturing experiences, dreams and fantasies of the author.

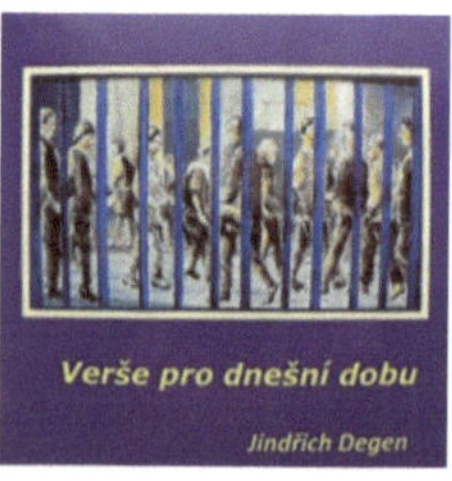

Verše pro dnešní dobu (Contemporary Verse) is a selection of eleven works from *Volné verše*, presented as a graphically illustrated colour version. The verses speak to us today as much as in the time they were written.

ABOUT PATHWAY PUBLISHING

Pathway Publishing (www.pathway-publishing.org) is dedicated to sharing truth and beauty through books, as well as websites. It aims to present what is true to life and reality, as well as what is edifying and inspirational. The goal is to provide sound information and to lift the human spirit.

Pathway Publishing has a vision of helping readers on their path of enlightenment and spiritual transformation. The wisdom and experience of spiritual teachers, thinkers, and visionaries from various backgrounds and faith traditions are recognized and valued. Books produced by Pathway Publishing include:

- *Artistic Inspirations: Paintings of Jindrich Degen*, arranged by Eva and Alexander Peck (2011)

- *Colour and Contrast: Artwork of Jindrich Degen*, arranged by Eva and Alexander Peck (2013)

- *Faces and Forms Across Time: Artwork of Jindrich Degen*, arranged by Eva and Alex Peck (2013)

- *Variations: Art Exhibitions of Jindrich Degen*, arranged by Eva and Alex Peck (2013)

- *Nature in Art: Artwork of Jindrich Degen*, arranged by Eva and Alex Peck (2014)

- *Floral and Nature Art: Photography of Jindrich Degen*, arranged by Eva and Alexander Peck (2011)

- *Nature's Beauty: Art Photography of Jindrich Degen*, arranged by Eva and Alex Peck (2013)

- *Volné verse (Free Verse),* Jindrich Degen (poetry in Czech, 2012)

- *Verše pro dnešní dobu (Contemporary Verse,)* Jindrich Degen (poetry in Czech, 2011)

- *Divine Reflections in Times and Seasons,* Eva Peck (2013)

- *Divine Reflections in Natural Phenomena,* Eva Peck (2013)

- *Divine Reflections in Living Things,* Eva Peck (2013)

- *Divine Insights from Human Life,* Eva Peck (2013)

- *Pathway to Life: Through the Holy Scriptures,* Eva and Alexander Peck (2011)

- *Journey to the Divine Within: Through Silence, Stillness and Simplicity,* Alexander and Eva Peck (2011)

Some of the publications are also available as e-books.

For details of both books and websites, visit
http://www.pathway-publishing.org

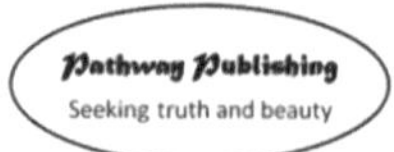